THE ROAD SCHOLAR

By Dr. Bob Winford

Copyright@2015 by Robert L. Winford

All rights reserved. No part of this book may be reproduced or transmitted in any form or by any means, including but not limited to, electronic or mechanical, including photocopying, recording, or by any information storage and retrieval system without express written permission from the author.

Library of Congress number: Pending

ISBN: 978-1-940752-65-9

These stories are true. Names have been changed out of respect for the individual's privacy. Any similarity to persons living or dead is purely coincidental. These stories are true.

Cover design and cover photographs: David Vinton

Copy Editor Cathy Lane

Original sketch photography by Bobby Brewer

Sketch by Kimberly Perkins-Murillo

Truth Book Publishers
Franklin, IL 62638
www.truthbookpublishers.com
877-649-9092

Printed in the United States of America.

A humorous and enlightening collection of stories of a man I've admired for years.

Surfer/Chaplain Chip Rohlke
Christ is Creator Ministries
Melbourne Florida

The Road Scholar is a delightful read that kept me anticipating the next adventure. You will find yourself enveloped in anticipation, intrigue, romance, and apprehensive all at the same time.

Dr. Margaret Hejhal
Educator

Recently I visited my native home in the Philippines and took a copy of *The Road Scholar* by Bob Winford. As I shared it with my family and friends I watched the expressions on their faces and immediately knew the book would be a success.

Lucille Padrita
INER Investments
Palos Verdes Peninsula, California

The Road Scholar is a great feel-good book. Knowing Bob Winford I can see his face and hear his voice in each episode. Filled with wit, charm, kindness, insight, and wisdom as well as projecting an amazing grasp of human nature, it's a book I treasure and you will too.

Dr. Kathy Lettieri, DPhil., CFLE
CEO, SolutionbyResolution.Com

Prologue

As a publisher of college and university e-books for the past twenty-five years, I know a successful book when I see one. The Road Scholar by Dr. Bob Winford could be a college text in the humanities, a must-read for psychology and other social science curricula. The stories encapsulate trust, values, and respect and at the same time turn ordinary situations into hilariously funny moments. Dr. Winford's style portrays human nature and the qualities of interpersonal relations in an intriguing way.

I predict this collection of true-life stories of Bob Winford will become the makings of movie scripts in the not-too-distant future. Their humor, romance, and edge-of-your-seat danger make this book an exciting read. They are the right prescription for renewing the spirit and reviving the imagination.

I have followed the life and professional career of Dr. Winford for many years. His wit and wisdom depict his unique understanding of the human spirit. His grasp of current national and international issues and his ability to articulate them contribute to his genius as a public speaker and radio and television guest.

Steve Mozena
E-book Publisher
Mozena.com

Walking the paths of The Road Scholar is like being with an old friend who shares life's humor, adventure, personal romance and dangers, as well as life's hopes and dreams. I know because I have walked many miles with Dr. Bob Winford and I feel at home with his kindred spirit. You will too.

Standing on stage with him at conventions, rallies, or gatherings of educators, waiting for my turn at the podium, gave me a sense of being in the company of a legend. His regard for others, his strong belief in the founding ideals of America, his respect for the treasured principles of freedom, and his loyalty make Dr. Winford an associate to remember.

Working with him on social or educational projects and issue and candidate campaigns across America, I can attest to the wisdom and integrity of my colleague, mentor, fellow author, researcher, and friend. Wherever Bob may be, in any given time, situation, or place, he brings with him a unique imagination, a superb presence of faith, a one-of-a-kind sense of humor, and an amazing understanding of human nature, which shines through in each of the short stories in The Road Scholar. These true stories depict actual life adventures, filled with Bob's antics, which have been displayed eloquently. They will touch your heart and bolster your spirit.

For more than half a lifetime, Dr. Bob Winford has been providing guidance and support as a political strategist and consultant to more than 725 political candidates. His skill as a photographer, writer, radio and television producer, campaign organizer, and public speaker puts him at the top of the list of people you want to listen to and get to know.

Talk about your next best read, The Road Scholar is expressive, deeply emotional, and real. Dr. Bob taught me long ago to share our gifts; here in The Road Scholar, he shares his.

Dr. Darin Martinelli
Founder and CEO of Strategic Wealth Advisors, LLC
San Francisco, California

Contents

The Journey 9
Love at First Sight 12
The Recorder 15
Met Any Chicks Lately? 17
Little People 19
The Quilt 21
The Paris Peace Talks 24
Shanty Town 26
Monte Carlo Romance 29
Writer? Wrong! 31
El Reno, Oklahoma 34
Colosseum in Rome 37
The Alarm Clock 39
George Wallace 42
Ship Shape 44
The Zap-In 47
The Vicious Dog 51
The Lighthouse 52
10 Downing Street 55
The Bag Man 57
The Bodyguards 59
John Doe 61
Buchs to Liechtenstein 63
Your Place or Mine? 65
The Baptism of Maude 67

Well, Excuse Me	71
The Border Guard	73
Waxing Eloquently	75
The Road Block	77
The Old Duffer	79
The Blizzard	80
Saint's Alive	82
Bridge to Andorra	84
The Swiss Chickhikers	86
Sidetracked	88
Party of One	90
Springfield Blues	92
The Gate Crashers	94
Miss America, Jon, and Norris	96
Sudden Death	98
Ricochet	99
No Tanks, I'm Full	101
The Cat Got My Tongue	103
A Voice from Above	104
Okay to Swim	105
Muffle It, Lady	107
A Rack of Bones	108
Speechless	110
My Mic and Dean	112
Hanky-Panky	113
Alone in the Dark	114
Hamming It Up in Spain	115
The Scout Leader's Pick-Up	116

Winning by a Nose	118
The Rainbow	120
A Left Hooker	122
A Snake in the Woodpile	124
The Blind Driver	125
The Wasp Attack	127
Sock It to You	128
Good Golly, Miss Molly	130
The Day Planner	132
Whiskey	134
My Big Gulp	136
One Hot Mexican Dish	137
Hello, World	139
Itching for Fun	142
Food for Thought	144
The Clip Joint	146
A Dog's Life	148
The Air Raid Warden	150
Marvin	152
Snake Handlers	154
Me and My Big Can	157
The Four-Word Letter	159
The Coal Minor	161
Barnyard Animals	163
Nightie-Night	165
Hits the Spot	167

THE ROAD SCHOLAR

By Dr. Bob Winford

The Journey

Airports, train stations, and bus depots are the loneliest places on earth. Everyone has a destination, or they have already arrived. People are rushing to their paradise, or this is it. Family and friends gather to see them off and wish them well, or they are here to welcome them home. But for me, these points of embarkation or disembarkation were lonely, even though they are crowded with excited people. There was never anyone to say hello or good-bye to me. No friendly hug, no admonition to be safe, have a nice trip, take care of myself, or most importantly, hurry back.

So, I injected myself into the tiny family of love or circle of friends who gathered over there to wish that guy well. It was easy to be him. My imagination had lots of experience in that regard. On lonely street corners, I could imagine a rush of pedestrians doing what pedestrians do. In an empty elevator, I could carry on a three-story conversation with myself. In a desolate hotel room, where voices could not be seen, only heard, I was suddenly the center of attention. But out on the street, where every passerby judged you, the conversations could only be in the silence of my mind. People would consider you a "nut" if you actually talked out loud as you walked along the street alone. I know that all too well.

But here at the train station, I wanted, more than anything, for someone to welcome me home, even if it was an act of mistaken identity.

I got off a plane one evening and saw all the excitement of another welcoming party. I hurried to the baggage claim area where all the limo drivers gathered, holding their placards with family or company names on them, waiting to pick up their fare. I spotted one driver holding a sign with the name Winston scrawled on it. He was my target. I walked toward him and said, "Let me get my bags first."

"No," he said, "that's my job. How was your trip? Did you meet any interesting people? Where did you stay last night? Let's see, you're coming from Miami, but before that, where were you?"

Dang, I thought, this is great. I felt like I met an old friend. I believed this guy was really interested in me, but, as much as I enjoyed all the attention, I had to end it.

Days later I caught myself thinking about the limo driver and how upset he was that he almost missed the "other" Winston. "Heck," he said, "I could get fired." He wasn't my friend. He didn't like me. This was his job. He was a pick-up with a limousine. I didn't matter to him and neither did Winston. It was just his job to pick up a passenger and take him from here to there.

Others don't really know lonely—not the lonely that builds up inside of you, but the lonely that is etched on your heart; the thick, weighty kind that is written across your face in bold letters. Most people who experience that kind of loneliness cover it up by rushing to board the plane, hurrying up the escalator, or pushing ahead of the crowd to get where they are going, to end up being the only person in another empty room. It's sad to be the world champion at life's game of solitaire. The roaring, thundering sound of silence is deafening to the desperately lonely.

If we could, for a moment, look back over our lives, we might see mountain peaks that stand high above the horizon—moments in our history that left great, positive impressions or indelible marks forever. Those mountain peaks are separated by valleys—places where we had to gather our wits, muster our will, call on our best spirit of commitment, or summon other energies to fortify us during our longest nights. Those peaks and valleys are the makings of our existence: building blocks of our character, the substance of our soul, the strength of our humanity.

There are so many mountain peaks in life: the day you fell in love, the day you graduated from high school or college, the important moment when your name was called and you knelt on the pillow emblazoned with the academic seal from your university and were bestowed with the doctorate you long sought. There are others: your first kiss, marriage, the birth of a child, or the sadness of death. Mountain peaks are those defining moments that give others a better understanding of you and you a better understanding of yourself.

These peaks have different meanings and value because most of them came at a great price. High school was a breeze, when you look back. It was one of those perfunctory things required of you because everyone in your family graduated or you were the first to do so. The other accomplishments, college and graduate school, were add-ons that seemed fitting for you to pursue, so you did.

Life has its mountain peaks. But the valley experiences, those forceful episodes, are what shape our character, sustain our dreams, show us our personal limits, and give us the courage to reach beyond our imagination.

Everyone likes a winner, a champion, a success story. But all the victors and all the conquerors reached the mountain peaks by trudging through the valley. The valley is where the tough battles are fought and won.

What makes you laugh? What entertains you? What energizes your being? What bolsters your hope? What gives body to your dreams? What imagery coddles and comforts you to sleep at night? What thoughts hurry the dawning of a new day? On your journey through The Road Scholar, you will experience my short collection of episodes that humored, romanticized, excited, encouraged, dazzled, and sometimes frightened me out of my skin.

The Road Scholar is a collection of stories that happened as I traveled throughout the United States, Canada, Mexico, the islands of the Caribbean, and nations of Europe. These travels gave me the opportunity to meet fascinating people and be at the right place at the right time.

Our journey, yours and mine, follows a winding path that often detours. These detours are what sprinkle our experiences with mystery, intrigue, and adventure. Occasionally, romance creeps into the picture and brings with it someone who makes unforgettable impressions or leaves lasting scars. True romance seems to be buffeted by both. Like bookends on a shelf, they support the novel, history, and how-to editions of life.

Let the journey begin.

Love at First Sight

Mile Marker 1,976

When you define life as a landscape of peaks and valleys, it makes it easier to understand how your history evolved.

But the fun times and the firsts in your life created their own mountain peaks on your horizon. Of all the firsts in my life, it was that first true love that added intrigue to my journey; so, let me tell you about her.

You may not believe in love at first sight, but I do! It is built on a matrix that has developed through the years. The beauty of your fourth grade teacher, the strength of your mother, the daily presence of the girl next door, and the waft of fragrance from the stranger that just happened by. All of these elements give shape to the woman who one day walks into your world. Suddenly, there she is: the living, breathing love of your life; the woman who will give a new rhythm to your beating heart, a new sparkle in your eyes, and a vibrant spring in your step. From the moment she appears, your existence changes forever.

Maybe you were at a favorite restaurant, the corner hurry market, or that spot where you rendezvous with your morning cup of coffee. You looked up and there she stood.

The news of the death of Dr. Belin, my mentor and good friend, was shocking. For many years, I saw him as invincible. I thought he would be there for the rest of my days. Now, he was gone and I was to give a eulogy at his funeral in Phoenix.

At the moment, I was a classroom teacher in a public school and asked for a few days off to attend the funeral. The substitute secured by the principal arrived a day early to go over my plans for class in my absence.

There was something special about her. But, by now, I was used to someone drifting in and out of my life. Those experiences were much like the shadows of a passerby that silently touch you without leaving as much as a trace. This time it was different. I heard her talking in the distance. Her laughter was melodious and contagious. There was a bounce in her step, even in her voice. When she walked into my room, led by the principal, I at once knew I liked her. Her presence filled the room, or maybe just the emptiness that occupied my heart. I had to get to know her.

I asked if we could talk after school. I wanted to fill her in on what to expect from the students and to discuss the lesson plans she would have to follow for the five days I would be gone.

I told her there was a restaurant called Coney Island a short drive from the school and I could meet her there when classes were dismissed for the day. Little did I realize, the restaurant was in the worst part of the city. It was bad enough this town was the murder capital of the nation; I picked one of the worst places in the area to rendezvous.

Talking with her that afternoon was amazing. She seemed politically conservative, which was important to me. She had a grasp of national issues, was smart, and was beautiful. What else could a guy want? It couldn't be better than that.

What was exciting about her covering my classes while I was out of town for five days was that when I returned, I would get to talk with her again to see how things turned out.

At our meeting, we talked about the problems she might face in my absence. I told her about the students who would try her patience. We covered the lesson plans and then we went our separate ways. That is, she went her separate way, but I couldn't get her out of my mind. At the airport I thought of her; on the plane I thought of her; when I landed in Phoenix—well, you get the picture.

The funeral was a sad and moving experience. Dr. Belin had been more than a professor I admired. He was a strong influence on my life and career choice. As a teacher, he was devoted to teaching and was always ready to respond to students' questions, help with research, or clarify points. But more than that, he was a friend. Now he was gone and I would miss him immensely.

The substitute teacher's name was Karen. Should I buy her a small gift from Arizona? First, I thought yes, and then I thought no! Gee whiz, she was being paid to substitute for me. Why would I buy her anything? What was this something that was eating away at my heart? Did I have a crush on Karen? There was no one to answer that question but me. No one even heard the question but me. Besides, she probably had other guys pursuing her. What chance would I have? How would a person like me ever get her attention? But why was she here? And more importantly, how could she, a woman I'd met just days ago, prance on my emotions the way she did?

I didn't know her last name, but I was already thinking about changing it. That was nearly a lifetime ago. After all these years, she still spells her last name the same way I spell mine and her aura still holds me in its grip.

The Recorder

Mile Marker 396

When you travel alone, as I have most of my life, you develop little techniques to keep yourself entertained or sometimes just to keep your sanity.

Note-taking is difficult when you're driving down the highway. So I bought an inexpensive handheld tape recorder to capture my thoughts and ideas, instead of having to remember them or stopping to write them down on a pad of paper.

But I discovered another use for the recorder. I practiced recording myself saying, "A cup of coffee, please." And my next message was, "Black!" I thought how funny it would be to see the expression on the waitresses' faces when I pretended not to be able to talk. How would they react? Would it work? Or would I laugh and give away my secret?

The next truck stop would be my first experiment. I took a seat at the counter and fumbled for my little recorder. When the waitress asked for my order, I pointed the recorder in her general direction and pressed the play button. "A cup of coffee, please."

She said, "Do you take cream?"

"Black" was the recorded reply. It worked. She brought me a cup of black coffee, but before she walked away she gazed at me for a moment. I knew she wanted to say something. I didn't know what to do. The only other things I had left on the recorder were "Check, please" and "Thank you." So, I scrambled for a piece of paper and pen and wrote, "You have a nice smile."

She put her hands on mine and said in a whisper, "Thanks. It would be nice to get to know you. I hope you come back soon." I felt stupid. Why do I do these things? She is just a wonderful lady, working at a job she obviously enjoys, and I come along with my dumb mind experiments that do nothing but entertain me.

She really believed I couldn't speak, that I was handicapped. All she wanted was to lift my spirits and wish me well. By the time

I finished my coffee, I had collected more than my share of smiles from her and a touch on the shoulder twice. She leaned into me, cupping my hands in hers again, and asked if I needed anything else. "Would you like a sandwich or some warm soup?" I shook my head no.

When I left the truck stop, I had a new take on things. Maybe I could learn more about people by using my new little recorder than I thought—not as a tool to entertain myself, but as a way of getting to know people, their attitude, their respect for others, and especially their regard for the handicapped.

I'm onto something, I thought. Often I would not have to pay for my coffee. The waitress would say, "That's on me," and wave me on. Later, on the road, I wondered out loud, "Who do they think recorded the message?" If I did, then why didn't I just order?

There are some really smart people out there working in coffee shops and restaurants. I don't mean to put them down. I have often questioned what I would do without these hardworking and uplifting men and women who do these jobs for low wages and often for long hours just to meet the needs of the public. My heart goes out to them.

Met Any Chicks Lately?

Mile Marker 582

About three hunger pangs south of Chicago is the most unforgettable chicken restaurant on the planet. As I vaguely remember, it was called the Chicken Hut, the Brooder House, or maybe the Hen and Rooster. I'm not really sure of anything except that their chicken was to die for. This haven for the hungry sat just off the old nationally famous U.S. 66.

When you entered, chicken symbols were everywhere: on the menu, pictured on the walls, emblazoned on servers' uniforms, and displayed in farm knickknacks sitting on the counter at the cash register's station. The chicken theme was backed by incredibly tasty food. The aroma in the air and the ambiance tantalized your taste buds and took up permanent residence in your mind. Once you've eaten their chicken and savored the atmosphere, you never forget the place.

I finished my delicious meal and, before getting back on the road, I went to the restroom. After sitting there a few minutes, I suddenly heard female voices. Hearing their chatter made me freeze. What are women doing in here?

I listened more closely to be sure of what I heard. They were saying things I really didn't want to hear. I didn't know whether to feel sorry for them or be angry with them.

I held my breath, wanting to just be done with my business and then get out. Finishing, I tried to get myself together quietly. I felt sure the women thought they were alone; in fact, I figured they probably had come to this restroom so the women they gossiped about wouldn't hear them. I knew that when I walked out of that stall, they would be shocked. But that's what they deserved, gossiping as they were.

I opened the door of the stall and headed straight toward the door. The women froze. Silence hung in the air. The women, who seconds ago couldn't talk fast enough, were now speechless.

I wanted to ask them what they were doing here, but I knew the answer and didn't need a response from any of them. I wanted to say something about needing some privacy but didn't. I just wanted to get out of there as fast as possible.

I glanced back at the restroom as I walked down the hallway and said to myself, "It's right there on the door! 'Hen,' just as I thought!" Across the hall on the other restroom door, the sign said "Rooster."

Then it hit me! What an embarrassment. I was wrong. I had been in the ladies' restroom all along! "Hen," shucks. I thought it said, "Men."

If any of you ladies remember that day, please forgive me. It really was a mistake on my part.

If you forgive me for my mistake, I promise not to tell any of the others about the naughty things you talked about that day.

Little People

Mile Marker 33,987

Room service usually isn't worth the wait, or at least I don't enjoy sitting in my hotel room hanging around for someone to bring my sandwich and coffee. Eating alone sitting on the edge of the bed or trying to create a makeshift table out of the tiny desk is frustrating and pointless. So, I usually get dressed and hurry to the coffee shop off the lobby.

I was unaware that a convention was being held here in the hotel. With several people waiting at the door to be seated and seeing that the counter with its comfortable-looking seats was nearly empty, I claimed one and took my seat.

To me, there is nothing more satisfying than a full breakfast without having to go through the line at one of those miserable buffet tables with their plastic sneeze shields. Why is it that the largest people on the planet are always in front of you loading their plates and trays to the brim? Some can't wait to get on the other side of this gigantic food island, so they reach across the steam table for a morsel, in fear it will be gone before they get there.

I ordered my usual: two scrambled eggs, no meat, whole wheat toast, coffee, and occasionally orange juice. It was then that I began to look around at the conventioneers. To my surprise, they were all beautiful little people. Some would barely come up to my shirt pocket. I had never seen so many in one place.

During the convention, these delegates discussed issues of access, safety regulations, job opportunities, and especially legislation that protect their rights. I have much respect for groups and organizations that are willing to work collectively for the good of their causes. The little people's convention being held this week in this hotel took on those challenges.

Sitting at the counter with its elevated vantage point gave me the opportunity to survey the attendees. Some had arrived much earlier than me and were lined up at the cashier to pay their bill.

When I finished my last cup of coffee, I climbed off the stool and took my place in line with them.

As I neared the cashier, I noticed there was a three-step platform in place, which led up to the lady manning the cash register. Great idea, I thought. When it was my turn, I saw the riser caused me to stand several feet just out of reach of the friendly and gracious cashier, so I mounted the steps, too. How embarrassing to be so high. I had to lean way over to give the lady my guest check and cash. As I turned to go down the steps of the riser, I saw I was the center of attention. Everyone was looking up at me. Should I say something? Was an apology in order? I didn't know what to do. Then one of the kind gentlemen grinned and broke into laughter and said, "This guy is one of us. He's a member of the family. At heart, he knows we are all the same height. I like him."

What an amazing comment for him to make. These people will always stand tall in my eyes.

The Quilt

Mile Marker 1,061

As I got back on the road, I hurriedly focused on my mission: to deliver an important message to a minister's wife in a town halfway between Chicago and St. Louis, Missouri. I arrived in Springfield, Illinois, and found the church. The secretary directed me down the hallway and pointed to the door where the quilting club was meeting. "The minister's wife will be in there," she said.

On the door was a placard that read "Faith Community Quilting Club." I stood for a moment taking in the simple message. I had never heard of a club where putting together quilts was such an important venture. Did people actually gather to quilt? It seemed like a dull project grandmothers would undertake, not something so interesting that you would form a club. Besides, who would join such an organization? Maybe I was making too big a deal out of it. After all, I was here to deliver a message to the minister's wife—a five-minute side trip in an otherwise normal hectic road trip.

Through the door, I could hear the sounds of women busily socializing, but more than that, they were putting together a work of art. Their friendly chatter made me envious of just twenty minutes of their time. Their weekly visits together were so disarming, so friendly, full of hope and warmth. These ladies know each other. They respected their friendship. What would it be like to have a small band of friends you've known forever? My "friends" weren't like that. The people who populated my life were just individuals who happened to be there: business acquaintances, an occasional fellow worker, maybe a tagalong, but never one who really fit the description of "friend." What I wouldn't give to have the camaraderie of mutually respectful people with which to interplay during life. I often thought someday I would end the road trips, settle down, live in one area for the rest of my days, and have friends. But for now, I need to see her, deliver the note, and get on my way.

My knock on the door was met with "Come in." As I walked

in, I was impressed with the size of the room. It was much larger than I had imagined. In the middle was an oversized table that was covered nearly side-to-side with a white, bedsheet-like fabric. The women were sewing together squares of various designs and attaching them to the white under-fabric. They looked up from their work and, without missing a stitch, carried on their conversations. I said, "I'm here with a note for the minister's wife, but I don't think I know who she is."

I was curious. The ladies all seemed occupied with their part of the project but at the same time interested in my sudden appearance at their "quilting bee." "I've never seen such a thing as this in my life," I said.

The pastor's wife stood and introduced herself and said, "What? You've never seen quilting done before?"

"Right," I said. "Tell me about it."

She said, "The club makes quilts and sells them to support their sick and shut-in visitation mission. The club members visit lonely people and, to cheer them up, take a small gift of flowers or a fruit basket."

I delivered the note to the minister's wife and told the club members how much I appreciated the special work they were doing.

As I left the room and walked slowly down the hall, it hit me. Their patchwork quilt was so much like my life—small parts that seemed incomplete in themselves but sewn together form a completed whole. There was not a single thread that passed through every piece of the ladies' quilt; they were all just stand-alone pieces each attached to the common sheet.

Was this a description of my life? Am I nothing more than a patchwork quilt to warm a body on a cold night? Am I just a thin barrier to ward off the chill in the air?

Glenn, a lifelong family friend and one of the great influences of my life, once said, "Bobby, today you are the result of every decision you have ever made." I thought about that statement again. I had no idea how my life was shaped by the choices and decisions I made through the years. Little did I realize how small happenings had shaped my thoughts and ideas. These experiences and episodes were like the patchwork squares of the quilt.

My life may be a patchwork quilt, but there is one significant difference. There is a single thread that runs through all the days of my life from my earliest memory until now. That single thread is my faith, a moral fiber that connects every moment of every day and represents itself in my beliefs and conduct. My faith connects me to the higher power, the Almighty Creator, who was and is the Genesis of our existence.

The searching spirit that dwells within all mankind reaches out to touch the Divine. Those who believe there is more to all of this than our brief assignments on earth, long for a greater knowledge of the Divine. I'm beyond the question of the existence of God, the Father of all. One day, years ago, my faith stretched out its hand and touched the spirit of Him. It felt good. More than that, I felt assurance, for the first time. In that one encounter, I became aware that He resided within me.

The Holy Scriptures came alive and meaning jumped off those historical pages and into my everyday life. His majesty is everywhere. The earth, rivers, oceans, mountains, deserts, and every place we turn, there is more evidence of His existence. Look at the animal kingdom and the gift each is to mankind. Then humankind, with its genus, is the great likeness of the Creator Himself.

What shapes us and makes us more than the sum of pieces quilted together? The answer is in how we share our talents, ideas, ambitions, hopes, fears, dreams, faith, and life itself.

The Paris Peace Talks

Mile Marker 3,444

On January 15, 1973, Nixon announced a suspension of offensive actions against North Vietnam. The United States Secretary of State Henry Kissinger and Tho, the leader of North Vietnam, met on January 23 that year and signed a treaty, basically ending America's involvement in the war. The agreement was signed by the leaders of the official delegations on January 27, 1973, at the Majestic Hotel in Paris. I was there. Not at the meeting, but on the streets of Paris, just across from the Majestic.

The Majestic was built as a hotel, but was not used for that purpose. It sits a stone's throw away from the Arch of Triumph and Rue des Champs-Élysées, the famous and most expensive shopping avenue in Paris. The week of the Paris Peace Talks, I hung around the Majestic. I knew what was going on inside and wanted to be as close as possible to the making of history.

The hotel was under the watchful eye of Paris police as well as agents from the participating nations. Sections of metal fencing were connected together to form a barrier to keep intruders away from the building. Many police cars and other security vehicles were on site to prevent access to the parking areas. The negotiating team was made up of key members of a variety of governments and their safety was of utmost importance. Every precaution was taken to maintain security.

Each day in the early morning, limousines would pull up to the entrance of the Majestic, and members of the negotiating team would go inside. The security guards were on alert, and it was difficult to get a good look at who was arriving. English editions of newspapers reported the talks, and I followed the happening with keen interest. I read the news accounts each morning at sidewalk cafes before taking my vigil at the Majestic.

What was significant about being there was the development within me of the importance of being aware of national and international issues. These talks, especially, were vital to the future relationships of the countries meeting in Paris. Each nation played a role in the negotiations.

Of major concern to the United States was how to exit the conflict in Vietnam and do so with the least amount of damage to the prestige and influence of our country.

Secretary of State Henry Kissinger was a skilled negotiator, but he was also suspect of having a more liberal view of world affairs. He was believed by some to be a strong and persuasive advocate for one-world government, a policy subtly advanced for many years by liberal political and business leaders. One-world government is a view I strongly oppose.

The ugly scars of Vietnam have never completely healed. I often wonder where we would be if the Paris Peace Talks had failed or never occurred at all.

Lessons of the Vietnam conflict should have been learned, but, evidenced by conflicts and wars being waged today, we learned nothing. Thousands of American men and women, as well as troops from nations allied with us, have been killed, as have tens of thousands of people native to Iraq and Afghanistan. It is time to weigh the result of conflict before we commit our troops and prestige. What do we expect to gain from our involvement? What price will we have to pay for these expected results? Are we helping to instill freedom, democracy, and peace?

Shanty Town

Mile Marker 449

Traveling the country playing bass fiddle with a successful musical group is as exciting as it gets. Our team, the Gospelaires, represented a Christian college in St. Louis, Missouri, and worked to attract new students to the school.

The Gospelaires appeared in conventions, convocations, churches, camp meetings, and rallies in Minnesota, Illinois, Ohio, Missouri, Iowa, Virginia, North Carolina, South Carolina, Georgia, Tennessee, and Kentucky.

In the Appalachian Mountain area near Corbin, Barbourville, and Harlan, Kentucky, many of the families lived in poor, substandard houses. Some of the houses were little more than tarpaper shacks. The scene was gripping and made a lasting impression on me. I was only seventeen years of age, and seeing other young people living in these conditions was heartbreaking.

These families subsisted on the barest of necessities. The men worked the coal mines, and the women worked to stretch their meager income and provide the best for their families in the endless struggle to make ends meet. Clothing was a hand-me-down garment passed from the oldest child in the family down to the next of age. I caught a glimpse of this poverty on weekends during the school year back in St. Louis, Missouri, and witnessed the hardship of poor families trying to survive from day to day.

On Saturday evenings, students from Pentecostal College were expected to minister to the needs of street people. In those days, these homeless people were called bums, hobos, tramps, or vagabonds.

Shanty Town, an area of St. Louis along the Mississippi River, was home to many of these poor people, who shared makeshift living quarters—lean-to buildings that were nothing more than shipping crates nailed together to give some shelter from the worst of elements.

Donny and I would take another student or two, for protection, as we visited Shanty Town for gospel meetings. Neither Donny nor I were preachers, but we could read a scripture, give a brief witness, or at least go through the motions of sharing our story with these less fortunate people.

On one such Saturday excursion to the river's edge, Ray went along. He brought with him his new flash camera. His was a film camera that had a device mounted on top to accommodate a flash bulb that would create a burst of bright light and illuminate the scene to make picture-taking possible. He had several extra flash bulbs for photographs that night.

Some of the Shanty Town attendees were handicapped, or we thought they were, and demonstrated various behaviors that sometimes were frightening to inexperienced college students like us. We were not wise to the ways of street people.

We asked the congregants if they had special needs or things they wanted us to pray about. Then one of us would lead in the prayer, a brief three- or four-minute period of time when we recited a well-known prayer from the Bible and continued by mentioning the special needs of those present, often recalling the exact requests that were made.

We didn't have regular church furniture, just a hodgepodge of odd chairs, a music stand, and a few song sheets.

This was Donny's night to lead. For his opening, he asked if there were any requests for prayer. He said that he believed the Lord would answer our prayers if we prayed in faith. Several had important things they needed and Donnie listened carefully to each one. Then he had all the attendees kneel at their seats while he led in prayer. His booming voice sounded full of authority, and I actually believed God heard him. I know the neighbors did because some of them shouted for us to quiet down. When Donny finished with a rousing "Amen," one man jumped to his feet and shouted, "It's a miracle! As I had my eyes closed over here praying, I saw this great burst of light. It was the brightest light I ever saw in my whole life. It seemed to go from one side of the building clear over to the other side. It was a miracle, I tell you. Brother Donny, what does it mean?"

I had to listen to this. I couldn't believe Donny was going to explain the flash camera and Ray taking pictures to a man who thought he just witnessed a miraculous bolt of lightning tear through the building. I thought to myself, This is going to be fun.

Okay, let's look at the facts: We were in a church where there are people who had many, many needs. The three of us were there to witness to the congregants that there is a God who loves all of us no matter what our station in life may be and we just asked if anyone had a need in their life. Whatever those needs were, we were going to pray that God would meet them right now. During the prayer, Ray took a few photographs with his flash camera. The man who saw the "lightning bolt" had no experience with flash photography, and Donny was going to explain that the prayer we all prayed had nothing to do with the lightning. Good luck, Donny.

Monte Carlo Romance

Mile Marker 11,207

The rooftop restaurant at Monte Carlo's famous Hermitage Hotel gave a breathtaking view of the Bay of Monaco. Large, privately-owned luxury ships and yachts filled the harbor. One luxury yacht sported two helicopter pads.

You could see perched on the cliff across the bay the magnificent palace of Prince and Princess Rainier. Floodlights bathed the palace and you felt you were in a fairyland among the wealthiest people on earth.

In the late 1950s, Grace Kelly and Prince Rainier were married. The wedding was celebrated by the television and movie industry as the social event of the century. The list of invited guests included heads of state, the greats of Hollywood, and the highest members of Europe's social circles.

The news media focused on every detail of the event and gave it front page billing in major newspapers across the United States and the world.

Now, Karen and I were here in Monte Carlo enjoying the ambiance of a culture that is only a dream in our homeland.

It was August 3. Karen surprised me with a special birthday dinner out on the rooftop of the famed Hermitage Hotel. It was elegant. The restaurant's wait staff made us feel we were the most important guests they had ever served. At the close of dinner, just as we were finishing desert, the sky lit up with a magnificent fireworks display. High in the heavens overlooking the ships moored in the harbor, the burst of brilliant lights filled the sky. Watching each rocket explode and then flutter back to earth was exhilarating. Each burst was amplified by its reflection in the bay and the thunder of the rocket's explosion echoing against the mountains.

I thought Karen arranged all of this and I wondered what it cost. I was afraid to ask. Then the waiter told us that in the month of August each year, several countries are invited to enter a fireworks competition. At the end of the month, a winner would be announced.

This night it was Italy's turn and, in my opinion, they were certainly in the competition. Round after round of brilliant rockets zoomed into the sky and, as they burst into beautiful patterns, created a breathtaking sight. As I looked into Karen's eyes, I thought, This is a fairyland and I'm living a dream come true.

Although she had not arranged this extravaganza, it was not out of the realm of possibilities. She had the ability to turn small family events into the most heartwarming occasions imaginable. So, as we left the magnificent rooftop dining area, I had a feeling deep inside that this would be an evening I would cherish for a lifetime.

It couldn't get any better than this: an extraordinary dinner, a mind-boggling fireworks display, and now I was walking out of the building into another Monte Carlo night holding the hand of the one who forever holds my heart.

Writer? Wrong!

Mile Marker 6,331

As I boarded the plane, I noticed a young attractive lady looking at me as though she knew me. She had walked past my seat in the waiting area several times. At one moment she hesitated, and I was certain she was going to approach me. If she did, I would at least be able to find out how or if we knew each other. I have a problem remembering names. Was she the daughter of a family friend? Maybe she's related to a candidate or officeholder I worked with in the past, or maybe she's just a total stranger.

In a hurry to get my carry-on in the overhead bin and get buckled into my seat, I put it all out of my mind. I was surprised when she ended up being seated right next to me. She sat in the center seat, a young college-aged man sat in the aisle seat, and mine was at the window.

When we took off, she turned her attention to a novel she was reading. Midway to Phoenix, she glanced up and said, "I don't want to be forward, but I think I know you. That sounds like a come-on, but there is something so familiar about you."

I had been looking at the book she was reading and noticed there was no photograph of the author on either cover or on the inside where they usually give a brief biography of the writer. The author was very popular and I remembered seeing several of his works. "I don't think we've ever met," I said.

Her comeback was clever, I thought. "My name is Gloria. Let me pretend I already know yours. It will make our conversation more fun." She returned to her book and in a moment she looked up and said, "Oh my goodness. Yes, you wrote the book I'm reading and half a dozen others that were my favorites. I knew it," she said excitedly. The name she called me was very flattering. It was a new one for me. I have been mistaken for the lawyer who represents famous Hollywood stars, a popular television host, and at times even a questionable politician, but never such a prominent writer.

I put my finger to my lips in a gesture to ask her to talk softly. She lowered her voice and in a whisper said, "It's such an honor to be sitting next to you on this flight. Are you staying in Phoenix for a while?" she asked.

I said, "No, actually I am going to have to hurry to catch a connecting flight."

As soon as we landed, I would make a mad dash for the next gate. I knew that would get me away from her in case she stumbled onto a current book with "my" photograph in it. "Will you please autograph my book?" she asked.

I said, "Yes, tell me your name again." As hurriedly as possible, I scribbled a note to her and in a huge flourish scrawled, "Your friend," and scribbled my new name. Then things got worse.

She said, "I think I have read all of your books. Which one pleased you most?"

What could I say? I didn't know any titles of this author's works. I had not read any of them. I didn't have a clue. It's not a good thing for an author to be speechless, but I was. Awkwardly trying to come up with the right words and hoping for a believable answer, I said, "I can't talk about it, but the one I like the most is the one I am working on right now. Just to give you a heads up, I've always wanted to include a fellow passenger in one of my plots."

Her unforgettable smile let me know she would not pursue the conversation further. As the plane landed, she was kind enough to let me go ahead of her. When I got to the concourse, I bolted for the exit. I had my carry-on, so there was no need to go to baggage claim. I wondered almost aloud, "Why do I get myself into these things?" She was a pleasant, beautiful person who did not deserve to be misled. But I am hit on so many times by a lot of people who think they know me, I often play along just for the fun of it. Going along with them makes the time pass faster, and on the way I meet some very special individuals.

I've been accused of being everyone I am not. "You are that talk show guy on television?", "You are that attorney who represents the famous stars in Hollywood?", or "You are a politician?" No, I'm not any of those people, I am just me, but if you insist, you can call me any name you like.

I've thought about her often. She has a book that I autographed. What does she tell her friends? Has she seen her favorite writer on television and wondered why he looks so different in real life?

El Reno, Oklahoma

Mile Marker 39

There was nothing unusual about the hitch rail outside the sheriff's office. After all El Reno, Oklahoma, was part of the Wild West and, since the local lawman rode a horse, it was only natural he would tie up his horse in front of the jail.

If there ever was a real Matt Dillon, he had to be the sheriff of El Reno. This man was tall, wore one of those ten-gallon hats, carried a scary-looking six-shooter, and kept the town safe from outlaws. During my days in El Reno, I didn't witness any shoot-outs at the corral, but if there had been any, I'm sure this sheriff would have won.

Everything about this part of Oklahoma was Western. The summer days were hot and dusty, and nights were cool. Rodeo posters were nailed to trees and placed in store windows. Cattle shows and Western events were the popular attractions, but the current attraction was the big gospel tent down at the city park, just across the railroad tracks.

The sign out front in bright red letters read "Evangelist Clifford Thacker Preaching Nightly! This Week Featuring Music and Singing by the Thacker Trio."

He was no D. L. Moody or Billy Sunday. Some thought he had a touch of Elmer Gantry's flamboyance. One thing was for sure: He was not a run-of-the-mill preacher either.

His sermons mesmerized the audiences. As he walked back and forth on the wood-plank stage carrying the microphone, stand and all, the eyes of the congregants were riveted on him. They were enthralled. Every now and then the audience would let out a loud and robust "Amen!" Their engaged attitude was an encouragement to him. The evidence of their love for his sermons was the fact that the crowds grew larger each evening. Soon the tent was packed and every seat filled. On several nights, the attendance was so large that those who came late had to stand outside.

The Road Scholar

The part of the sign that bothered me most was "This Week Featuring Music and Singing by the Thacker Trio." Actually, the "This Week" part wasn't exactly true. I was one-third of the trio, Warren and Joyce were the other two-thirds, and we were there for the duration of the El Reno Crusade. When he had the banner painted, Mr. Thacker must have thought people would rush out to the meetings to hear the Trio, thinking they would not be around next week. Then the part of the sign that referred to the Thacker Trio wasn't true either. There wasn't a Thacker in the bunch, not one. Joyce wasn't a Thacker, Warren wasn't a Thacker, and I was not a Thacker. I had, in fact, picked up a nickname, Hawkshaw, or Hawk for short. Last name of Thacker? Nope! We were just three oddly matched young people who played accordion, guitar, and bass fiddle. We could sing, but our singing wouldn't make us famous. Joyce played accordion, Warren played guitar, and I played bass. Together, we were three musicians, three singers, one trio.

During the day, Warren and I would adjust the ropes, reset the tent stakes, and, if it rained, make sure the water hadn't pooled in the parking lot or run under the tent creating mud puddles or making the sawdust aisles a soggy mess.

The gospel meeting started at 7:30 p.m. and lasted until about 9:00 or 10:00 p.m., depending on how long people lingered or how many lined up for special prayer for healing or other needs. Once everyone was out of the tent, Warren and I would close the tent wall curtains, rearrange the chairs, pick up any trash that had been discarded, and, in general, make sure the place was tidy for the next meeting. Then we could go to bed.

Our sleeping area or "bedroom" was on the stage of the tent cathedral. I would set up my army cot behind the organ near the back edge of the stage, and Warren slept across the stage beside the grand piano. One naked sixty-watt light bulb was left on through the night. The bulb was hanging from one of the massive center poles near the top of the tent. We thought it would attract bugs and keep them away from us as we slept. It didn't, but it was some comfort to know there was enough light for us to see, in case someone came in during the night to vandalize the place. No chance of that, though. This was a peaceful little community where everyone

35

knew everyone. Then, too, the sheriff with that beautiful horse of his could be on the scene in short order.

El Reno, a small Oklahoma town, about thirty miles west of Oklahoma City, the capital of the state, is one of the real Western communities. Living in El Reno for even a short period of time gives you a sense of belonging. The part of El Reno where we put up our tent was more than a mile off the famous U.S. Route 66, so we didn't think we would attract any riffraff, hitchhikers, or troublemakers heading west. We were wrong.

It must have been near midnight when the rustling sound jolted me awake. I sat up quietly and looked around. Back near the edge of the tent, I could make out the form of a man. I hoped my mind was playing tricks on me, but when I turned toward Warren, he was awake, too, and startled at the sight. At the other side of the tent, three or four men were building a fire in the middle of the aisle. Our job, through the night, was to make sure no one bothered the equipment on the stage or anything else in the huge tent.

The old saying, "They are more afraid of you than you are of them," didn't comfort me at all. Warren and I were frightened out of our skins, but we had to take some kind of action. We couldn't let these guys build a fire under the tent. There was a danger the whole place would go up in flames.

I hurriedly put on my shoes and tied them. My hope was that Warren would be ready to run, too. Then I jumped up and said, "Hey, you can't build a fire here; these are restricted grounds!" What the heck did that mean? I wasn't sure, but I repeated in an even louder voice, "Hey, you can't build a fire here; these are restricted grounds!" It must have worked because they stomped out the fire and left without a word.

The next morning one of the neighbors told us some of the drifters saw the tent as a welcome sight in chilly or rainy weather. That didn't make me feel any better, but at least I knew these men were not going to be a lasting problem. They had most likely just happened by and thought they would take refuge in a dry tent for the night.

You know everything turned out all right or I wouldn't have lived long enough to tell you about it.

Colosseum in Rome

Mile Marker 8,739

This was my seventh trip to Rome. During all these visits, I found myself drawn to the Colosseum. This magnificent structure of engineering genius, built by slave labor, was designed to seat thousands of spectators. The entire audience could exit the arena in a matter of minutes. How amazing is that?

Once inside, you can let your imagination take control. The roar of the crowd, the ferocious lions and tigers, and the blood bath caused by the battles between man and beast conjure up the most frightful sights.

On this trip, I planned to spend a few days photographing the Colosseum inside and out. While you can buy photo collections, I think nothing replaces a personalized photographic tour.

Standing several hundred yards away gives you a sense of the immense size of the structure. This is the view you are presented with in a picture postcard display of this historic monument. However, once inside, it is important for you to have some knowledge of the history of events held here and understand the horrors of those days.

I arrived at the Colosseum early in the day and spent hours investigating, probing every corner, looking into every cubical and room. The building is fragile. The flooring is gone and much of the stone has been plundered or removed for structures elsewhere. A good mind's eye helps to see the seating areas of the arena and to visualize those dreadful sporting events of yesteryear.

You are tempted to pick up a souvenir stone or pebble to take along, despite the posted warnings prohibiting you from doing so.

After more than four days crawling over as much of the Colosseum as is humanly possible and shooting hundreds of photographs, I decided I now had the most extensive collection of pictures of this historic place and it was time to leave.

On the train from Rome, I fell asleep. When I awoke, I discovered some of my things had been stolen: my jacket, a tour book I'd been reading, and the fifteen rolls of film I had spent so much time shooting. The replaceable stuff was no big loss, but the film was lost forever and could not be replaced. Amazingly, the memories of those incredible days will linger in my mind forever. The experience is internalized and nothing can take that away.

The Alarm Clock

Mile Marker 2,583

I was drawn to Memphis because this year it was the host city of the biannual gathering of the national religious organization to which I belonged.

Ellis Auditorium was replete with banners welcoming delegates from all over the country. On display were posters marking the locations of various committee meeting rooms and lists of convention hotels as well as directions to a variety of restaurants within walking distance.

I chose not to attend the morning or afternoon business and organizational meetings because I learned long ago the same old "cream of the crop" inventory of elders would be appointed or re-elected to fill the vacancies created by the usual game of musical chairs that has existed for as long as I could remember. Occasionally, a newcomer would be groomed to fill a leadership role if he "fit the mold" or was one who would toe the company line. I was neither.

So, I spent my mornings and afternoons catching up with associates I had not seen for two years. I wanted to know how they were faring and what they had been doing and, most of all, learn what new ventures were on their horizon. I held these little briefings in area coffee shops or hotel lobbies.

One day, as I walked the main street leading away from the Ellis, I decided to stop at a department store that housed a great soup kitchen in its basement. It was one of my favorite haunts in Memphis because the soup was to die for.

In the lower level of this amazing department store was a fabulous restaurant, more of a lunch room than a dining room. I sat at the counter where I could see the gigantic copper soup kettles that contained the soups of the day. My guess is the chef started making the soups in the early morning. The kettles were about four feet in height and nearly sixteen inches in diameter. They each contained a different soup. My favorite was bean soup with bite-sized chunks of ham. My taste buds told me somewhere there were tiny bits of onion, some indescribable seasonings that altogether made this the most remarkable lunch on the planet. The soup, complemented with a slice of homemade bread with fresh creamery butter, made my stomach ask for seconds. Thankfully, my mind overruled.

While I sat at the counter finishing my lunch, I noticed a gentleman seated nearby looking at his watch. While I was not close enough to see the hands on the watch or detect what time it was, I was reminded that my small Memphis mission was to buy a new alarm clock. Mine had given up telling me the accurate time several weeks ago and that was not a good thing.

Walking down the main street led me past some of the city's elite shopping stores. One that featured fine ladies' clothing and accessories had a new gimmick to attract women into the store. They had some kind of atomizer that sprayed a fine mist of ladies' cologne into the air each time a customer opened the door. I thought it was one of the cleverest ideas I'd seen or heard of in a long, long time. Any man with good sense would have walked briskly past the store for fear his wife or lady friend would wonder where he'd been and with whom. I didn't linger.

Besides, I was on a mission. I needed a dependable alarm clock. I'd recently been to London, England, and was wondering if I could find a miniature clock like Big Ben whose chime could be heard all over the city. While I didn't want to wake sleeping guests in the next rooms at my hotel, I did want to wake at the appointed hour so I would always be on time.

In my walk, I soon came upon a store whose windows were filled with household items: cookware, brooms, vacuum sweepers, and dishes. I was certain they had clocks.

The stores in those days were not like the big-box stores of today. They actually had salespeople who ran various counters. All you had to do was find the right counter and you were in business. I found the lady standing at the clock counter and told her what I wanted. I needed a nice, small alarm clock that could be depended upon to wake me at the right time every morning. Behind her were dozens and dozens of boxes housing alarm clocks. The search was on to find my clock. The first box she opened had a beautiful clock with a dark face that made the white glow-in-the-dark hands stand out. "That's the one for me," I said. "But wait, the clock says it is now 4:32. I want one that is accurate. It is now nearly 1:00 in the afternoon. I want one that is factory set for the accurate time."

She explained that the clocks were not running right now and all she would need to do is wind it up and set the correct time. I wasn't happy. I told her these clocks all came from the factory and I'm sure the factory sent them out in working order. Several minutes later, she had opened more than a dozen boxes and no clock had the current time.

About then, the store manager happened by. Seeing all the open boxes with all the same model clocks sitting on the counter, he said, "May I help you?"

When I told him I wanted a clock that came from the factory with the correct time and in working order, I thought he was going to laugh. He didn't know I was having a little fun with the clerk and I was not about to tell him. I said, "Sir, this clock"—holding one up in my hand—"says it is nearly 2:00. I'll tell you what I'll do. I'll go down the street and have a cup of coffee to kill a little time. By the time I get back, this clock will be as close to the actual time as possible. When this young lady completes the sale, it should be the exact time. Can the clerk set this clock aside for me?"

He said, "Yes, but we have a coffee shop on the second floor, and you will be my guest for coffee. Follow me."

41

George Wallace

Mile Marker 3,621

During his 1972 presidential campaign, George Wallace visited Michigan. His plane landed at Flint's Bishop International Airport. Wallace and his entourage arrived at Atwood Stadium and proceeded to the stage prepared for his appearance. The press bus pulled up in front of the stadium, and photographers and members of the press began to get off. After nearly all of the press had disembarked, someone said, "Hey, hold on. We got off the bus too soon. This is not where we are supposed to be. The stage area is inside the stadium."

Hurriedly, they began to get back on the bus. I was walking past the bus just as the confusion broke out. I joined in and said to anyone within earshot, "We're all right. We just need to drive around the corner and down to the rear of the stadium to get to the stage area."

"I think you're right," a photographer said. I seized the moment. This was my chance to get up close and personal in the Wallace event. I climbed aboard the bus with the rest of the press and rode to the stage area. This is really cool, I thought as I stood with the press and other photographers busily getting into position for the best photographs. I tried to make my cheap camera as inconspicuous as possible. My heart was racing. I thought to myself, I just crashed this party—well, not a party, but an important political event. When I left home, my best guess was I'd be one of hundreds of onlookers far back in the bleachers listening to a presidential want-to-be. But instead, I was right up front, within arm's reach of the podium, with all the press people, getting a firsthand look at a special time in history.

The moderator finally got to the line everyone wanted to hear: "Ladies and gentlemen, let's welcome our guest today, the next president of the United States, Governor George Wallace."

With the thunderous applause of the audience, their loud roar of approval, and their welcome cheer, I thought any moment the band would breakout with "Hail to the Chief." Governor Wallace stepped to the microphone and launched into his speech. It was no secret—from the response of this crowd, Michigan truly loved him. Wallace wowed the audience. He was an energetic speaker and had the heart of the crowd in his hand.

As he was finishing his remarks, I looked for a way to get out of the stadium without having to board the bus. The press was going to head to the airport and I could not do that. The long walk back to Atwood Stadium would be many miles, so the trick was to get out of here now. Just as I was planning my exit, one of the journalists cornered me and said, "I don't know where you were sitting on the plane on the flight here, but I need you to do me a favor. I ended up sitting by an absolute nutcase and I won't do that again. When we get back to the airport and board the press plane, please save me a seat." I assured him I would do my best and left before they started boarding the bus for the airport.

On my way back to my car, several people stopped me and asked questions about Wallace, the plane trip here, where we were going now, and how they could get involved in the George Wallace campaign. Luckily, I got through an embarrassing situation and finally home.

Little did I realize, within days, George Wallace would be shot at an event in Laurel, Maryland, and his chances at the presidency would not just be short-circuited, but would end forever.

Ship Shape

Mile Marker 4,862

Within minutes after boarding ship on a crossing from the New York Harbor to South Hampton, England, the captain of the SS France sent his aid to my state room and requested I come to his quarters. I was uneasy. I thought I had done something wrong or did not have my documents in order. When I arrived at his quarters, I was shown in and introduced to the captain. He said I was to speak at the nondenominational, nonsectarian religious service on Sunday morning. I was shocked. A world-known evangelist was on board together with his evangelistic team. Why would I be asked to fill such an important responsibility? I said, "Sir, there are others on board who are much more qualified for this assignment."

"No," he said. "You will do nicely. Let my assistant know what we can do to help and give him your topic so we can publish it in the ship's daily newspaper. Many passengers will want to attend." I agreed to stay in touch and returned to my stateroom, wondering all the way what in the world I could say on Sunday morning that would interest such a diverse audience.

The days hurried by and Sunday was approaching sooner than I wished. I had given the captain my topic and requested a musician to play the piano or organ for the service. I was told it was all arranged and was asked for a short list of songs for the service. I selected old favorites: "Amazing Grace," "All Hail the Power of Jesus Name," and "Just as I Am." I had selected the twenty-third psalm as my reading and outlined several relevant thoughts for my homily. The service was to be held in the ship's theater, a huge auditorium that seated several hundred. It had a balcony for first-class passengers that hung well over the main floor. It was not possible for the tourist-class passengers seated on the first floor to see any of the first-class passengers in the balcony above them. It was my observation that the ship was designed to keep separation between the first-class and tourist-class voyagers.

On Sunday, I arrived several minutes before the scheduled starting time. The musician would be arriving soon and I wanted to make sure we were on the same page, so to speak. The back entrance to the theater led up a steep stairway to the stage where I would speak. As I stood there in the wing, just out of sight of the audience, I noticed, to my surprise, there was not just a pianist or organist, but a small gathering of musicians who played in the ship's nightclub each evening. Four men sat in the space between the front row and the stage, one with a saxophone, one with a violin, another with a guitar, and the forth man sat at the piano. I descended the stage steps and walked through a narrow door to speak with the musicians. They were excited with the song selections and said the audience would probably know the songs and would sing along if I led them. All I needed was something else to fret about. There were no hymnals or song sheets, and I thought things could not be worse for me, when the violinist said he had made several copies of the songs and would ask one of the attendees to pass them out if I wished. I wished! He did. I went back up the steps to the stage and with a hand motion signaled the audience to stand. The musicians started the beautiful "Amazing Grace" and the service could not have been more moving. All went well. Tourist class sang their hearts out, and their enthusiasm drowned out the silence of first class, which is usually the case.

There was no lectern or stand where I could place my notes. My notes were in my pocket and I was too embarrassed to take them out. I would have had to hold them. I was sure I would be trembling, drop them, or make some awkward blunder, so I just left the notes in my pocket. After all, I thought, I had written them and surely I could remember what they said. Through the years of speaking before large and small groups, I made it a practice to commit to memory as much of the structure or framework of my speeches as possible. I learned to know my opening and closing "by heart," as my mother would say, and have several points I could focus on for the body of my speech.

For years, I had given thought to talking to and with audiences. If there were several hundred people seated in front of me, some would say you have an audience of hundreds. I always thought of it as having hundreds of audiences of one. If I could talk as though I was talking to just one person and focus on communicating to one person, the hundreds would take care of themselves and my message would resonate. It became easier to build rapport with the audience when I developed a one-on-one relationship.

At the conclusion of my homily, I motioned for the audience to stand, and, as if on cue, the musicians started the final song, "Just as I Am." Before I dismissed the audience with a prayer, I told them I would be available offstage to talk with anyone who had a question or concern. As the people left the theater, the musicians continued to play. When the seats were all empty and the young man who had passed out the song sheets returned them to me and left, the violinist said, "We have to take this show on the road." I took it as a compliment and felt a little warm inside.

When I got back to my stateroom, there was a message under my door. I opened the envelope and read the captain's words: "Thank you for such a wonderful job. It's an inspiration to have you on board. Come and see me when you have a moment." I didn't go. I was afraid there would be another assignment.

The Zap-In

Mile Marker 4,582

That Friday, I was in Minot, North Dakota, staying at the city's finest and best hotel. To my surprise, the Miss North Dakota Pageant was being held that weekend, and my hotel was hosting the event's staff and contestants.

As I walked through the lobby with my camera slung across my shoulder, a beautiful young lady approached me. She said, "Sir, are you a photographer?"

I said, "Yes, I am."

She continued, "Are you staying at this hotel for the weekend?" I said I was. At that point, she introduced herself as the director of the Miss North Dakota Pageant and asked if I would be available to meet with her and her staff in the hotel bar at 2:00 p.m. I said I would. I had no idea what she wanted; I just felt a little awkward about meeting in a tavern. I had never had an alcoholic drink and really didn't know how to handle situations like this. As it turned out, their photographer was in Zap, North Dakota, photographing and reporting on the Beer Bash going on there. Rumor had it students, as a joke, planned to go to Zap and camp out for the weekend. The fun event turned into a major problem for the residents of tiny Zap, some forty miles northwest of Minot.

As we sat in the bar, the director told me what she knew about their missing photographer and why she needed me to shoot pictures of the pageant this weekend. We talked about the program schedule and the presentations the contestants would be making that evening.

But first, she told me the troubling story of why the media and, in particular, their photographer were in Zap and would be unavailable to get to Minot for the Miss North Dakota event.

The National Guard had been called into Zap, and the town was in lockdown until they could get things sorted out. A riot had broken out and a lot of property damage had occurred. Troublemakers, mostly from out of state, had been involved in drunken brawls, and near mayhem prevailed until the situation was brought under control.

It seemed students had been planning their camp-in called Zip to Zap for some time. What was expected to be a few students having fun turned into a serious disruption of Zap's community life and the trashing of their town. Initially, police were called in to assist in helping restore peace and usher the rabble-rousers out of town. Hours before dark, the visitors drank the town's two bars dry; beer and other drinks were brought in by the carload.

Hundreds of people from all over the country rushed to Zap to get in on the excitement. One person said, "I don't think I ever saw so many motorcycles in one place." The people, mostly hippie types, gathered and boozed it up through the night.

On a normal day, Zap is host to less than three hundred souls, and its only "business district" includes the two bars and combination eateries. You can walk from one edge of town to the other in less than six minutes.

The Zap-in was the forerunner to Woodstock, which occurred later in 1969. It is reported it all started when a bored student newspaper editor up in Grand Forks wrote an article promoting a Zip to Zap weekend. Not to be outdone, students from other parts of the state joined in promoting the event, and the Zap-in was born.

Zap was populated with reserved, conservative residents and was the most unlikely spot for a hippie sit-in. When the booze was gone, one of the bars was torched and burned down. At that point, the citizens demanded the gathering break up and the visitors leave town.

On Saturday morning, the National Guard took control of the situation. By this time, the troublemakers had long gone and the remaining students were either sobered up or were not among the drunk rabble-rousers in the first place. The cleanup, damage to property, and crushing blow to community pride was costly. Who would pay for the trash removal and the hundreds of man-hours it took to restore the town? It's not known if a bill was ever sent to the students or if the students made restitution. One thing is certain:

The Road Scholar

Zap, North Dakota, and its beautiful residents did not deserve this invasion.

Well, I accepted the invitation to be the Miss North Dakota Pageant's photographer and hoped the photographs I took would be satisfactory. I had never had such a major photo assignment, and on such short notice, so I was more than a little apprehensive.

With my acceptance, the group decided to order a round of drinks to celebrate. I was not in my comfort zone; more than that, I had never had a drink in my life. I watched and listened as each person at the table placed their order. My plan was to order a soda or juice. Most of the drinks were alcoholic and had exotic names and I knew they were not for me. That is until the lady next to me ordered a pink squirrel. I thought that's it. It is simple; I can remember that name and it for sure would not contain alcohol. Besides, I was next. "I'll take the same thing, please," I said.

The waiter said, "A pink squirrel, sir?"

"Yes, please, a pink squirrel." I could tell by the stares I had said something wrong.

When the drinks came, I shuttered. There it was, all frilly with a pink umbrella no less. Oh well, I didn't drink it and soon excused myself to go to "another meeting."

The shoot went well. I was backstage while the contestants readied themselves for their various performances complete with costumes. Contestants had a variety of costumes; one was dressed like an Indian princess, others an oil well, a bail of straw, and anything that represented North Dakota and its many industries, cultures, and landscapes. Hundreds of photographs later and I put my camera away for the evening.

My schedule on Monday took me to Pierre, South Dakota, where I dropped off the twelve black and white rolls of film at a local photo shop and ordered one print of each. There was no rush service in those days, but luckily, the shop owner did the work himself and I had the prints before I left the area.

But there was a dark side; I did not have the name or address of the pageant director, so I carried the glossy prints of the Miss North Dakota Pageant in my suitcase for months. I still have them in my file cabinets, years later, and have wondered if I will ever come across someone who remembers that event and can give me a name or telephone number so I can get these treasures to the rightful owners.

While Zap was a disaster, Minot was an occasion of the heart. The dedication of these fresh, beautiful, energetic visionaries and their hope for the future of America made the North Dakota Pageant unforgettable. Here I had a view of the amazing American spirit unlike anything I'd ever seen.

The Vicious Dog

Mile Marker 8,397

Karen and I arrived in Vienna, Austria, and set out on our trek to the famous Schönbrunn Palace, the summer residence of the Austrian emperor's family. We had heard much about this historical home but had never had the opportunity to visit and take in its splendor. This would be our day! We walked along the street running beside the train station and noticed a suspicious-looking man and his huge dog coming toward us.

As a kid, my closest friend was my dog. I never really knew what breed of dog I had, but that didn't matter. She was mine and we loved each other. Dogs never have bad days or get out of sorts. At least, that's my experience with them. When you come home, they don't remember being scolded or anything negative. They are always happy to see you and come running up, wagging their tail. I learned a lot from Buzzie.

But the man and his dog in Vienna were a different matter. When we crossed the street to get out of their path, they crossed the street heading right toward us. Karen and I looked at each other. She said, "Are you thinking what I am thinking?" We were both afraid we would be attacked. Since we had no weapons, no umbrella, and nothing to use in defense, we were unable to protect ourselves.

I quickly hatched a plan. I told Karen if the scary man and his huge dog lunged at us, I would ram my fist down his throat and she should grab him by the testicles and hang on for dear life. Together we could render him harmless. Karen said, "That's a good plan, but what should we do about the dog?" We both roared with laughter and peacefully went on our way. I'm sure the man and his dog were more afraid of us than we were of them.

The Lighthouse

Mile Marker 8,397

They called her Sister Bucher. While I didn't know her first name or background, I learned a lot about her in a short period of time. One thing I detected almost immediately was that she was in charge and she wanted everybody to know it.

She was raised with a heart of compassion for the down and out. Alcoholics, drug addicts, the homeless, and the neglected were all her family. Her mission was to open a refuge for these people and all who needed a kind word and a hot meal. Lighthouse Mission stood as a beacon of hope and comfort on the edge of Kansas City's thriving business district.

This Mission was hers. Every day at 5:00 p.m., Sister Bucher stood in the doorway of the dining room and welcomed "her family" to supper. The fixin's were sparse: northern bean and ham soup, bread and creamery butter, ice water, and coffee. The coffee was stout but with no lingering aftertaste you might expect from a warmed-over brew at a C-rated coffeehouse across the state in St. Louis. After supper, her guests were directed to the basement of this old church building where they could freshen up for the nightly gospel meeting in the sanctuary.

The main sanctuary was on the first floor of this stately old house of worship, and in its day, it was one of the most beautiful church buildings in town. The gallery or balcony wrapped around the sanctuary and added extra seating for the crowds that gathered. Local singers and musicians, many of whom have gone on to television and stage fame, shared their ministry of music free of charge. The vagrants and vagabonds, the drunks and dropouts, the lost and lonely took solace in this cathedral of hope, a refuge for the weary and destitute. The music and singing soothed their worn out and raggedy lives. It seemed nowhere else could they find a place of love and forgiveness like the Lighthouse. To the downtrodden, the Lighthouse was more than a bright beacon in a dark world; its magic turned their nightmares of fear and anguish into dreams of hope and purpose.

This soft Sister of Faith had a tough side. If you ate from her kitchen and nourished your soul at the Lighthouse altar, you could stay the night in the basement dormitory and make a pledge to turn your life around.

It was unusual that I would be invited to speak at the Lighthouse for a few nights. I was not a recovered alcoholic nor was I one who had beaten the habit of smoking, but there was that side of me that believed in that positive human spirit that always reached for a higher rung and a brighter day.

I accepted the invitation and drove nearly 250 miles from St. Louis to Kansas City in a borrowed car, a 1940's Pontiac. The brakes "went out months ago," I was told. I'd never heard of brakes going out—maybe wearing out, but not going out. Whatever, I would take care of that. After all, I was borrowing the car, so the least I could do was have the brakes fixed.

I didn't. I didn't have enough money to buy gas for the trip and pay for having the brakes fixed, too. Instead I drove the whole distance to Kansas City with no brakes. Well, I did have the parking brake, a lever I could pull and activate the brakes in the rear wheels. Pulling the lever didn't bring the car to a stop, but it would slow it down within a few hundred feet.

On the highway, I would anticipate having to stop, then put the car in a lower gear, let up on the clutch, and the engine would slow my speed. That worked for the highway, but once I got into the city, things were different. I got into the right-hand lane and pretended to be having car trouble. I drove as slow as I could and still stay in the line of traffic.

When I arrived and parked my car on the side street next to the Lighthouse, I breathed a sigh of relief and considered my safe arrival some sort of a miracle, or as some might say, "the luck of a fool."

Sister Bucher and her helpers showed me to my quarters. I learned later her helpers were a couple of recovered drunks, dedicated to doing odd jobs around the place. My room was in the bell tower of the church. It was comfortable enough. After all, I was alone and didn't require much space, so this small room would do. I hung my clothes in a makeshift closet and sat my suitcase on the floor near the window. There was no desk or place to sit and read or write, so I used the dining room on the first floor.

Privacy was a forgotten word around the Lighthouse. Wherever you went, there were men gawking at you or offering to help. I learned quickly not to accept their offer, because there would be strings attached. They wanted money for cigarettes or booze, or they'd settle for just a single cigarette; I had neither. The routine was simple enough. To be alone and have the time to quietly think, I'd walk the mile or so from the Lighthouse to downtown Kansas City. One of my favorite hangouts was a little coffee shop near Twelfth Street and Vine. I visited it often.

There are not enough Lighthouses or Sister Buchers in the nation to help all of the downtrodden, but I am thankful for those we have. Maybe if we just promised to take care of our own family or those nearby, we could—in our own small way—be a lighthouse in someone's misty storm.

10 Downing Street

Mile Marker 8,397

    The Shaftsbury was my favorite hotel in London. It was small by American standards but had a quiet, tranquil atmosphere and an ambiance fitting to a loner. A television parlor off the main lobby, tables for two in the dining area, and a reading space set off by itself; a place to be alone; a place to think.

    London, an intriguing city, has a history of survival, and all the wonderful sights pay tribute to that survival: the Tower of London, the British Museum, House of Lords, and Westminster Abbey, and countless other historical sites.

    Plying the Thames River in for-hire boats from London north for a few kilometers and back gives you a look at the area from a different point of view. Riding under the famous bridges, past the businesses, brownstones, and piers, awakens one's imagination to life in England in a new way.

    Buckingham Palace with its pomp and gallantry was more than a day could embrace. The fact that London is still standing, with its history intact, is a testimony to the tough British spirit that doesn't take defeat nor allow the demise of centuries of treasured accomplishments.

    I was free in those days to roam the city at will and take in all the sights. Bobbies carried no guns; security by today's standards was nonexistent. I visited all the noted sites and events including Westminster Abbey, London Coliseum, Royal Opera House, Piccadilly Circus, Oxford Street shops, Harrods department store, and the Notting Hill Carnival. By the time you sat and watched the tourists gaze at the gates, guards, and glitz of British majesty, you had time for nothing else.

    Looking out the window of the coffeehouse told me it was a typical London day. It was raining, but not hard—just a drizzle. I had finished my muffin and coffee and wanted to take a stroll to see Downing Street again. This time I would not just walk past but would try my hand at knocking on the stately black door of Great Britain's most distinguished home. It was emblazoned with a beautiful and impressive gold number ten.

Of all the fascinations I had with the British Commonwealth, 10 Downing Street was at the top of the list. It was as accessible, in those days, as the nearest park or pub. Day and night, there was a lone guard standing sentry at the front door. For that matter, he could have been a statue fresh out of a museum dressed in his pomp regalia; there was pageantry written all over him.

Standing there in statuesque splendor was the usual British guard. My plan was to ignore the guard, snobbishly approach the door with an air that I belonged, and see how far I could get. After all, he couldn't shoot me, I thought. It worked. I stepped toward the door and reached out to knock when it suddenly opened and two gentlemen, busily talking, walked out. Somewhat apologetic, one said, "Excuse me," and stepped aside.

As the door closed behind them I said, "Would you mind to snap my photograph? Today is somewhat historical for me."

He took my camera and snapped a picture, thanked me, and both men disappeared toward Parliament Street.

I didn't have to knock. I had what I wanted: a quick glimpse inside, notice by the butler, and a photograph to boot. The guard paid no attention to me, and I wondered if he would have even attempted to keep me from knocking or entering the building had I tried.

I tucked my camera beneath my coat and continued my walk in the drizzle, wondering where I could get out of the rain quickly to write a few notes about my day.

The Bag Man

Mile Marker 1,298

The knock on the door surprised me. Who would be here at this hour of the night? I thought. It must be after 9:00 and I'm in the middle of an important film-processing job. I don't have time for visitors. I answered the door in my pajamas. There was no time to change, but why should I? "Tom, Cheryl!" I exclaimed. "What brings you to my part of the world"? If I hadn't sounded so friendly, maybe they would have kept going. "Come in," I said. They did. "You caught me in the middle of processing some film, but I'll only be a minute. Excuse me while I run down to the darkroom and switch the negatives in the film tank to the fix," I said, as though they knew or cared what I meant.

"Have a seat," I said. I rushed to the darkroom. If I hurried, I could make the switch and have time to load three more rolls of film. Timing myself through the years, I knew I could load a roll of 35 mm film onto the spool in seconds. So, if I really hurried, I could get all three rolls loaded, put them into the tank, and get back to Tom and his bride in short order. Then I would have seven minutes before I would have to pour off the developer and pour on the fix. Good work: It was done, and now back to my guests.

We made small talk for a few minutes, mostly about the weather. "Tom, this will be my last trip to the darkroom for forty minutes," I said. "When I return, we will have some refreshments." I put the film into the fix and knew that I really had a couple hours if I needed them, but I wasn't about to tell that to them.

"Can I get you something to drink?" I asked. Before they answered, I said, "I have cola, grape, orange soda, and maybe some root beer." They both wanted cola. When I opened the refrigerator, my eyes landed on the ginger ale. I took them their colas and went back to get something for myself. The pale yellow ginger ale gave me an idea. I grabbed a small plastic sandwich bag from the cupboard, held it open, poured about a half cup of ginger ale in, and sealed the bag. Quick thinking told me the surgical tape was in the medicine cabinet in the restroom. I taped the bag to my bare stomach and covered it with my pajama top. Taking a plastic drinking straw from the counter, I rushed back to the living room and joined my guests.

Cheryl said, "Aren't you going to have something to drink?"

I said, "Sure," pulled up my pajama top, ripped the plastic bag of ginger ale from my stomach, punched a hole in it with the straw, and began drinking.

Tom lurched forward and said, "By golly Bob, we're going to be late getting to the babysitter. We've got to go." They left and never came over again. The film turned out okay and the ginger ale wasn't half bad either, but being alone again was the best.

The Bodyguards

Mile Marker 6,439

The year was 1953 and I was back in Kansas City, Missouri, speaking at youth rallies. My daily routine included walking as many miles as possible, spending time studying at the local library, and people watching at local coffee shops.

It was at a coffeehouse I had one of the most embarrassing moments of my life. Finishing my coffee, I decided to go back to the library and take up where I left off with my research project. As I walked out the door, the glare of the bright noonday sun blurred my vision for a moment. I wasn't paying attention and ran squarely into a gentleman as he approached the restaurant entrance. We were both several feet from the doorway when I hit him. Immediately, a man caught me by the arm and stood me up. Another man helped the gentleman I had run into. It was obvious neither of us was injured. The man I hit was shaken but not hurt, and I was red-faced with embarrassment. I apologized and asked if he was all right.

The stern looks from the two men with him were frightening. They didn't seem to think it was an accident. There was good reason for their concern; the gentleman I ran into and almost knocked down was the former president of the United States, Harry S Truman.

His car was parked at the curb, and he arrived at this coffee shop obviously to have lunch. I didn't immediately recognize him, but as soon as it was clear to me this was President Truman, I was shocked. I mumbled some sort of incoherent apology and tried to gather my wits and retain some dignity as I walked away.

It was later I realized how much trouble I could have caused myself. By today's standards of presidential security, I would have been subdued, restrained, detained, questioned, and much worse.

I didn't talk about the incident for a long, long time. Today, I look back and wonder why security was so lax. Maybe it was the times we lived in, unlike today when the whole world seems to be gripped by a lunatic spirit where anything can happen and does. In these days, you can't be too guarded.

John Doe

Mile Marker 19,087

The explosion ripped apart the Murrah Federal Building in Oklahoma City, killing 167 men, women, and children. Millions of people in the United States and the world were rocked back on their heels when the story broke across the media.

A bright yellow rental truck loaded with fertilizer—a chemical that, when triggered, would result in a gigantic explosion—was driven to the front of the building. Its driver allegedly armed the device and walked away. When the device was detonated, it set off a nationwide hunt for the perpetrator.

News reports indicated there was a John Doe Number One and a John Doe Number Two. The public was quick to join in the search for these suspects.

Daily broadcast kept the story alive. Because this devastation was the talk of the nation, it was difficult to keep young children from hearing about it. All over the country, people turned in tips of having seen a suspicious-looking individual. Although authorities traced every lead, it seemed the two John Doe characters would never be caught.

One day, Karen and I took our eight-year-old daughter and her ten-year-old cousin with us shopping. In line to check out at a neighborhood office supply store, the kids were looking at literature on an adjoining table. Both kids crept close to Karen and whispered to her. They had important information on the "Oklahoma City Crooks." They even knew where one of them lived.

Tugging on Karen's arm, they urged her to "come here." As Karen neared the table they had been looking at, she saw under a glass tabletop a sample credit application. It was filled in with the sample name, John Doe, and a made-up street address, city, and state. "Look, there is the information the police are looking for. You'd better call them right now," our two new, young detectives said.

We hurried through checkout and rushed to our car. The kids were beaming with excitement about their discovery. We explained—well, that is, Karen explained—that while the kids' keen interest in solving the case had in fact uncovered what appeared to be some vital information, the store had mistakenly used the name John Doe in their sample application. We said someone should talk to the store owner about this and maybe suggest they use a different name since the police were hot on the trail of two men they were calling John Doe Number One and John Doe Number Two. In the meantime, Karen said, "We should all continue to keep our eyes and ears open for any information that might help solve this case."

Since Michigan was allegedly the home of some of the suspects in the Oklahoma City bombing, we as a family were rightly concerned that the suspects could be in our area.

As a shocked nation mourned the loss of so many lives, the authorities—including the Oklahoma City police, the state police, the FBI, the Bureau of Alcohol, Tobacco, Firearms, and Explosives, and many related law enforcement agencies—launched a manhunt scouring every nook and cranny searching for clues that finally led to the arrest and conviction of the criminals.

Buchs to Liechtenstein

Mile Marker 13,329

The train from Zurich to Buchs runs through some of the most beautiful Switzerland landscape. Spring is the chosen time to take in the sights and smells of the Alps. The air is crisp; the stillness of the mountains, with their majestic heights, their daring slopes, and the warmth of the inviting coffeehouses, chalets, and restaurants, can fill a volume of memories.

Soon after the train pulled out of Zurich, it started to rain. Not hard, just a drizzle; the kind of slow weeping sky that brings with it the haunting melancholy that must have inspired Roger Miller to write the song, "The Last Word in Lonesome Is Me." That's the emotion that crept into my mind. This lingering feeling of loneliness stayed with me as I stepped off the train in Buchs—a tiny storybook Swiss village—and headed toward the station to catch the bus to Vaduz, Liechtenstein. The rain and mist created an eeriness that would not go away.

I boarded the bus and took a seat near the front. My rain-drenched clothes made me hope the trip to Vaduz would be short. I wanted to get into a warm, dry hotel room and put this dreary day behind me. The bus droned on through the mist and fog. The silence hung thick in the air and was broken only when I finally got the nerve to ask the little old man beside me, "Do you speak English?" He sat there motionless and didn't utter a word. I looked around at the other passengers and no one made eye contact or in any way acknowledged my question. I had now resorted to having conversations with myself. As I got off the bus, I muttered something about how "friendly" everyone was. The fact is the passengers acted more like they were on their way to a concentration camp. Their blank stares, the deafening silence, their detachment told me they were uncomfortable with strangers, or maybe something more.

But finally, I arrived. Vaduz is a beautiful little town nestled in the foothills of the Alps in the Principality of Liechtenstein on the border between Switzerland and Austria. The home of the prince and his family, this capital city is proud of its appeal to tourists. As I trudged down the narrow street toward town carrying my suitcase, the depression lingered on. I looked forward to settling in for the night. It had been a miserable bus ride, but I was here now in this unforgettable fairyland.

Hotel Engel (pronounced Angel) was just around the corner. There it stood, a welcomed sight. As I entered the lobby and approached the desk, I said, "I'd like a room for one, please." The night clerk, who obviously had difficulty with English, stumbled through some remarks. She gave me my room key and pointed toward the tiny lift to the second story.

In my room was a bottle of water, a fruit basket, and a comfortable bed. That's all I wanted. Before I took a shower and climbed into bed, I stepped out on the little balcony and looked over the city. To my left, high in the hills, was a beautiful view. I thought it was a drive-in movie theater. I spent several minutes taking it all in. The "movie" didn't move. Maybe it's a sign, I thought. The next morning I inquired at the desk and learned it is the castle. "That's where the prince lives," she said. What appeared to be a movie screen was the castle flooded by huge lights. "The castle is visible at night for kilometers around," I was told.

I had roamed Europe for months and this was my tenth trip. With each mile and each new face, I fell more and more in love with the idea of living here forever. If I couldn't stay, the memories would reside in my heart, and it would only take a thought to revive the feelings I was having today.

Your Place or Mine?

Mile Marker 7,973

My good fortune of being able to travel all over Europe, the United States, Canada, Mexico, and the islands of the Caribbean has given me the opportunity to stay in some of the very nicest tourist homes, hotels, and motels on the planet.

I have a favorite hotel chain, with properties all over the world. I have stayed at more than 450 of their beautiful hotels. When you get familiar with the services, reasonable rates, quiet atmosphere, and enjoyable staff, you take the small challenges that come along with it with a grain of salt.

On four occasions, I rented a room that was already occupied. Late one night, after a particularly grueling day, I checked into my hotel and was given the key to the room. Carrying my one suitcase, I boarded the elevator and got off on my floor. The directions to rooms were indicated on a plaque on the wall as I exited the elevator. I followed the arrow and found my room. In those days, you were given a regular key with an attached plastic tag with the room number emblazoned on it. I inserted the key, unlocked the door, and entered. I fumbled for the light switch and sat my luggage on the floor.

It was then, in the darkness, that I heard sounds coming from across the room. I froze. "Who's there?" was the question the gruff voice uttered.

I said, "I must have the wrong room," and quickly backed out into the hallway. I looked at the key tag to check the number. I was at the right place, this was my room, but someone else was sleeping in my bed. I hurried back to the lobby and the night clerk and told him someone was already in my room.

Another encounter was not so friendly. There were a couple of people in my bed; they had rented the room and were not happy that I was given a key to their privacy. Neither was I.

It got heated. By the time I got to the night clerk, so did he.

Pointing his finger at me, he shouted to the clerk, "This man came barging into my room and embarrassed us. I should punch his lights out and yours, too."

I laid the key on the counter and showed the clerk that the key he had given me was the key to this man's room. I slept free that night and so did the other people. But saying that anyone slept that night is probably a big stretch.

Now I know how the three bears felt when they had that encounter with Goldilocks. The gruff men were more bears than I am a Goldilocks.

The other two "your place or mine" encounters are not for public consumption, at least not here and not now. The details are vivid examples of human nature and lend themselves to the makings of a movie. Watch the silver screen for the secrets of the other two keys.

The Baptism of Maude

Mile Marker 1,119

Maude was in charge of a congregation in Hamilton, Illinois, just across the Mississippi River from Keokuk, Iowa. Her parishioners called her Sister Maude. I was invited to conduct a series of meetings for her congregation. At the conclusion, there would be a baptismal service in the shallows of the Mississippi River, the border of the two states.

Keokuk was a small and friendly town of ten thousand souls, more or less, and hosted several short-order restaurants famous for counter service. I always enjoyed sitting at the counter on one of those round plastic-covered stools. The waitress scurried between the counter and the ever-busy short-order cook manning the grill.

Everything in Keokuk was within walking distance: the post office where transients like me called for their mail at the general delivery window, the haberdasher, the grocery store, the dry cleaner, and my favorite hangout, the coffee shop. Through the years, I have dubbed practically all eateries "coffee shops."

The meetings at Sister Maude's church began to pick up momentum. At least, the attendees were not ready for the meetings to end. "Can he stay a few more days?" they asked Sister Maude.

Her response was, "What happens, happens." But in the middle of the first scheduled week, she asked me to stay on for another week and I agreed.

She talked about the baptismal service as though I would be participating as a helper. The fact is I had only witnessed a few of them and had never actually conducted one myself. So, I was more than a little apprehensive at the thought that I would be one of the principals helping conduct it.

Saturday morning arrived and with it a real surprise. Sister Maude called me into her office and announced I would be in charge of the baptismal program, and she, too, would be baptized. She informed me that in the confusion of accepting the leadership of the Hamilton, Illinois, congregation, the clergy had not asked her about baptism or much of her background. But why would they? She looked every bit the part of a leader of a religious order. She had silver hair set in finger waves all over her head. They must have been permanent, because she looked the same every day, never a hair out of place. Her daily attire was white, from head to toe. She was decked out with a white dress, white stockings that had a beginning but seemed to have no end, white flat-soled shoes that gave her a solid footing, and a white shawl. Her shoes were the flat lace-up kind that gave her huge frame support. My guess is that Sister Maude fought problems of being overweight all her life, and fought a losing battle at that.

Now, it was nearly time to get the baptismal service underway. A ragtag bunch of bystanders gathered and blended well with the congregants, families, and friends of the baptismal candidates. A tall, slim man who stood near water's edge could have passed for a relative of the "Who me?" character you see on postcards at off-the-beaten-path truck stops. If I had to venture to guess, I would say several years ago he outgrew the shirt and pants he was wearing. He carried an accordion slung across his shoulder. As soon as he got it in position, he began to play "Shall We Gather at the River." A small band of believers near the front joined in singing, and soon it seemed the entire shoreline was alive with chorus.

An elderly gent waded into the water up to his knees, turned toward the singers, and began directing them. As he waved his arms, more and more people joined in singing. As the volume grew, I thought they could rival the best high school glee club in town.

Across the river, two fishermen sat in their boats and cast lines in the water. This was a favorite spot for anglers, but the threat of rain put a damper on their Saturday morning plans. I really think the handmade sign announcing "Water Baptism, Noon Saturday" posted at the entrance to the drive to water's edge and the sounds of singing had more to do with the sparse gathering of fishermen than anything.

The gentle breeze carrying the aroma of nearby dead fish caused some of the ladies in the audience to put their hankies to their noses. They were probably thinking the shorter the baptismal ceremony, the better.

This was a Bible-believing crowd. Water baptism was not a matter of sprinkling the candidate with a few drops or pouring water over their heads from a pitcher. Baptism meant, to this congregation, total immersion; the believer would be plunged into the river just like John the Baptist did in days of old.

My dilemma was figuring out how to baptize Sister Maude—total immersion. I remembered the minister would hold the folded hands of the baptismal candidate and say, "I baptize you in the name of the Father, the Son, and the Holy Spirit," and then push the candidate beneath the water and lift them up again. I'd heard ministers briefly instruct the candidate before the ceremony to assist in the baptism by going down on cue and back up again. I had no such instruction period. The line of believers taking part that day ranged in age from ten years to middle age and in size from small child to full-grown adults. Sister Maude was very large.

I stood about fifty feet from the shore. Next to me was one of the elders or deacons of the congregation. He was there to assist me with the service. Things went well for a while.

One of the first candidates said he had heard this was the largest baptismal delegation the congregation had ever witnessed. The pressure was building.

The last in line was Sister Maude. She walked slowly into the water. By the time she reached me, she was trembling. She turned to face the shore, and as she did she whispered to me, "Don't drop me. I can't swim a lick, and I'm afraid of the water."

My heart sank. All that was standing between me and a manslaughter charge was a three-hundred-pound woman. What should I do? She apparently had been watching the others and followed suit. She folded her hands and covered her nose. I put my hand on hers and had barely recited the words, "I baptize you in the name of the Father, the Son, and the Holy Ghost," when she collapsed and disappeared under the water. Her arms and legs were flailing as she seemed to speed downstream. The dam was no more than a stone's throw away. This was a real crisis. If she went over the edge, my world would have come to an end with hers. I wanted to shout to the top of my lungs, "Dear Lord, help us!" but I didn't dare. It would have panicked the crowd and startled the deacon.

Sister Maude could be seen bobbing up and down as she drifted farther and farther downstream. Soon she would be out of reach. I lunged toward her hoping to grab her by the arm; no such luck. I lunged again, and this time I caught the toe of her stockings and held on for dear life. That slowed her. Together, the deacon and I pulled her back. She was still flouncing, red-faced and choking on river water as we led her safely to shore.

The onlookers must have thought some sort of spiritual experience was taking place and gave us all a round of applause and a hearty hallelujah.

Well, Excuse Me

Mile Marker 12,215

Finally, I felt at home even though I was a long way from the place where I hung my hat in the United States. I walked the streets of Vienna, Austria, in search of something to fill a couple of hours before I had to be back at the train station. Of course, it felt good to be here and enjoy the beauty of this city. The history of Austria and the role these amazing people played in World War II is enough to saturate your mind with incredible images for a lifetime. How would that war have ended without the unbelievable feats of courage exhibited by the brave Austrian souls?

As I walked through the main business district, I tried to guess what people were talking about or what they were thinking. Not about the war, I was sure. It was as though I was in an American city people watching. Most of the difference was the language they spoke and my inability to understand them.

I browsed through stores in old downtown hoping to expand my memory bank of things positive with the few remaining hours I had before leaving Vienna again. I happened upon a wonderful coffee shop in the basement of a large department store. It reminded me of the old Smith-Bridgman's department store in Flint, Michigan, the town where I grew up. Well, there was one difference: Smith-Bridgman's coffee shop was on the mezzanine—but that's beside the point.

I sat alone at a table for two, watching people and listening to their animated conversations. The waitress came over and, I am pretty sure, asked what I wanted. I'd been in coffee shops all over Europe and thought I knew my way around. So with great confidence, I held up my thumb, which is the custom to indicate the number one, looked her in the eyes and said, "Un cafe mit krem."

"Entschuldigen," she replied.

"No, un cafe mit krem! No sugar!" I answered.

"Entschuldigen," she repeated.

"Look, ma'am, you can bring the sugar if you want to, but I don't use it and you'll just be wasting your time," I answered.

Later, on the train to Geneva, I told a fellow passenger this story. "Ha!" he chuckled as he explained, "She was politely saying 'Excuse me' and was going to go get your coffee. You hollered back an embarrassing remark. She ignored you and brought you your coffee."

I decided I'm one of those "dumb Americans" who gives our country a bad name.

The Border Guard

Mile Marker 8,397

I really love Canada. The beauty of the people, their love of family, their friendly nature, and their accent make them the ideal neighbor. After all, Canada is just across the border from my native Michigan, and I'm always excited when I get the opportunity to visit my Canadian friends.

Unlike some other foreign countries, where rude bureaucrats can rain rigid regulations on your parade that spoil your visit, Canada is like visiting a friend on a sunny day.

These thoughts filled my mind as I drove north. A popular Toronto church had invited me to share my European travel experiences, and I looked forward to it.

Driving all night from St. Louis, Missouri, put me at the Canadian border at dawn. It was raining and had been raining for several hours. All I wanted to do was hurry through customs, find my motel, relax tense nerves, and get some sleep in a warm bed.

I carried quite a few things in my car—my bass fiddle, recording equipment, projector, and an assortment of related and personal effects. The trunk held a variety of suitcases filled with clothes to last a lifetime.

I rolled down my window as the Canadian border guard approached. He asked the routine questions and then the killer one: "Have you been invited by the church organization to visit and speak of your foreign travels?"

"Yes, I have," I said.

"Do you have it in writing?"

"Yes, I do, sir," I said.

"Well, buddy, I'll need to see that invitation. Pull your car over there and get it for me," he said, pointing to a parking spot by the edge of the customs building.

I peered through the pouring rain and followed his pointed finger to the spot where he wanted me to go. "Look, sir, the invitation

73

is in my briefcase, in the trunk. It's raining and it will take forever to dig it out."

"I'll be here eight hours," he said, without missing a beat. I wasn't sure I felt the same way about Canada that I felt at the beginning of this trip. Then I reasoned, maybe he's not really Canadian.

Moments later, I stood at his window, soaked through to the skin, with the invitation in hand.

Waxing Eloquently

Mile Marker 6,681

    A member of the state legislature requested I stand in for him at an awards banquet. He asked me to present a certificate of achievement to a worthy organization on his behalf. After reading the remarks on the citation, I knew the presentation would be well received and quite moving for those affected.

    The Italian dinner theme had been executed perfectly, down to the finest detail. The servers had dressed the tables with red-and-white-checkered tablecloths and bright red candles, and they served spaghetti and meatballs—scrumptious food that I consumed with vigor and in volume. It did me in. I'd had a touch of the flu, but the pasta pushed me over the edge.

    Looking at my watch, I saw the time fast approaching for me to present the award. My stomach rolled and pitched like a ship caught in a storm, and I felt like a seasick sailor on his first voyage. I made a mad dash for the men's room. Rushing into a stall, I yanked on my zipper, need for relief building by the moment. The zipper was stuck and would not budge, no matter how furiously I tried to loosen it.

    Then I remembered my dear old mother's remedy. "Rub wax on a stuck zipper," she had said. "It'll work every time."

    No one provides restrooms with wax, of course, but I knew where to find some. Trying not to be noticed, I walked back to my table and, hoping no one saw me, slipped the big red candle into my pocket.

    When I got back to the restroom, someone was already in the enclosed stall with the door shut. As I waited for him to finish and come out, I started rubbing the candle up and down on my stubborn zipper. Just then a big burly guy from the table next to mine came into the restroom. He gawked at me struggling with the zipper and I rushed to explain.

    "Ah, my zipper's stuck," I managed to say gingerly, my face

turning red. He grunted something and quickly left. "Hey, come back here! I'll show you. It really is!" Too late, he was gone and so was my confidence and sense of dignity. Yet I had to fulfill my duty.

Now on stage, I stumbled through the awards presentation. All I could think about was what Mr. Burly Guy was thinking, and I could only imagine what he'd said to his friends at his table. "Hey, see that guy up there? I caught him in the men's room 'waxing his zipper.' Can you believe that? Mr. Awards Presenter waxing his zipper in a public john?"

I had gained restroom relief, but never did wax eloquent with my comments that night. It would have been better if I had kept my lips zipped.

The Road Block

Mile Marker 5,545

It was 4:32 p.m. Saturday afternoon when it suddenly dawned on me that I had failed to pick up my dry cleaning. My suits and shirts were hanging on the racks at the cleaners in a town sixteen miles away, and the cleaner would close at 5:00 p.m., not to reopen until Monday morning. Further, I was scheduled to fly home late Sunday evening. I had twenty-eight minutes to solve the crisis.

I jumped into my car and hit the road as fast as I could. If the traffic moved along at normal speeds and I had no traffic jams or other problems, I could make it to the cleaner in time. I was feeling better. I thought I'd pick up my stuff and be on my way back with ease.

But gnawing at my stomach was a tiny sense of anxiety. I had a feeling things might not turn out well. I was pushing the limit. Normally, I'd drive a bit slower, but the urgency of the moment ruled otherwise.

Ten minutes later, I found myself stopped at a traffic tie-up caused by road construction. Worse yet, I sat behind what seemed to be an endless line of traffic.

I pulled into the lane reserved for oncoming traffic in an attempt to get around the long line of cars. I felt the angry stares of their drivers as I passed. Just as I was about to get ahead of all the traffic, a road worker stepped in front of me. Now what am I going to do?

I looked around the front and back seats for something helpful and saw my passport on the seat next to me. I picked it up and opened it to my picture, which was next to the official United States seal.

"I've got to get through," I said, flashing my "official credentials" at the man. I wore a confident but concerned look on my face.

In a loud and commanding voice, the worker shouted to his road crew, "We've got a federal emergency here, guys. Let this man through."

Well, I got to the cleaners just in time, gathered my dry cleaning and laundered shirts, and hung them on the hooks in the backseat. Then I began my return trip, wondering all the while what I would tell the road crew this time.

By the time I got back to where the incident happened, the guys had all gone home. Only their abandoned heavy machinery sat on the road's edge ready for their use on Monday morning.

Mission accomplished!

The Old Duffer

Mile Marker 9,982

Have you ever been frustrated by one of those drivers who leaves his turn signal flashing but never turns? One day in Alabama, I followed a fellow like that, an old man driving a Ford. I watched him for a little while and wondered if he'd ever get to his corner.

Miles passed and his turn signal kept blinking, but he never turned; he never even looked like he'd be turning anytime soon. Finally, I couldn't take it any longer.

Just then I got a break. The oncoming traffic let up and I had an opportunity to pass him. When I finally got around him, I sped up to put some distance between us.

It was time to tell him his left turn signal was on. So, I turned on my left blinker and let it blink for a few seconds, then my right signal, and my left again, but to no avail. He didn't get the message.

Old people, I thought. God bless 'em. As I pondered the moment, I remembered it wasn't old people; it was mostly old men who never turned their signal off. Women are better at those things than men, I reasoned.

As we approached a small town, I decided to lose him and his annoying turn signal; it would be out of my mind forever. Right in the middle of this town, the city's only traffic light turned red and I stopped. I saw in my review mirror he stopped close behind me, got out of his car, and walked toward me.

I cranked down my window as he walked up. "What's your problem, sonny?" he asked.

"No problem," I answered, trying to be patient with him, "but your turn signal is on."

"Mine's on?" he snapped back, in his southern drawl. "You whippersnapper. Yours has been on for ten miles. I've been trying to tell you!"

How could I argue with that? I shrugged my shoulders in disgust and embarrassingly drove away.

The Blizzard

Mile Marker 12,841

The Dakota Lyceum tour took me to three or sometimes as many as five schools a day. Nearly every elementary, middle, or high school, religious school, college, and juvenile school had booked my lecture, "The High Roads of Europe: A Program about the Political and Social Lives of Residents in France, Germany, Italy, Switzerland, Austria, and Liechtenstein."

I visited every city, town, village, hamlet, crossroad, and watering hole in the Dakotas and loved every minute of my travels, even the long, long drives between schools.

Heading out for my first assignment of the day, I noticed there was a light snow in the air. My history of travel in the Dakotas let me know any light or moderate snow could turn into a violent blizzard quickly. This one did.

When I finished my last assignment of the day in New England, North Dakota, I realized driving would be treacherous, and, although it might've meant I'd miss the next morning's schedule, I checked into the only motel in town.

It was an unusual-looking place, a row of tiny mobile homes each housing two or three hotel-style rooms, but what a welcomed sight it was.

Before settling into my "plush" quarters for the night, I needed something to eat. Opening the door to a stiff wind, I stepped out into the heavy snow and tromped across the street to the combination bowling alley and coffee shop, ready for a sandwich and something warm to drink.

Even though I wore a heavy coat and scarf, I held the collar tightly closed with my gloved hands to stay warm. The cold biting wind took my breath away. Luckily the restaurant was less than a hundred yards away.

The few townspeople who were there commented on the weather; it looked like a real storm had settled in. The old-timers were the ones to listen to. They had weathered the worst of times and knew how to read the skies. The skill to survive the sudden changes in conditions was in their blood.

While I was at the coffee shop, I should have taken some snacks back to the room; little did I realize at the time that this snowstorm would paralyze the town and leave me stranded.

I slept soundly that night. The next morning I awoke to the hum of heavy machinery in the distance and discovered it was a snowplow. The driver was in the process of clearing a path through the snow that had drifted my doorway shut. In fact, the snow completely covered my windows and the front of my motel unit. As I opened the door, which swung in, I was faced with a wall of snow.

Hurriedly, I closed the door and sat down on the floor to ponder what I should do now. There was no telephone in the room, so I couldn't summon help. I knew I'd have to sit in my snow-prison until someone came to rescue me.

Since my front window was completely covered with snow and there was a wall of snow that sealed my exit, this was a huge claustrophobic moment.

At least the room had television. I turned it on to find it offered one show, a rerun of Bewitched—as in a single rerun. When the episode ended, I heard it rapidly rewind and start again.

Now, I think Bewitched is a charming show and I loved this episode. In fact, I had it almost memorized by the time I checked out. How many times can a fellow watch the same rerun while helplessly trapped in a motel without going nuts? Ask me.

After several hours, the kind and hardworking motel owner—and sometimes snowplow operator—cleared a path to my room. I walked through the snowy tunnel to the bright and beautiful New England, North Dakota, streets, wishing Samantha would wiggle her nose and clean the snow off my car!

Saint's Alive

Mile Marker 3,197

Every time I went "home" to Cape Girardeau, Missouri, Pastor Fred would ask me to go with him on his hospital and shut-in rounds. I loved it. We visited the sick and elderly, read scriptures, and mostly listened to lonely people talk out their frustrations and share their hopes of eternity.

One frail, older lady made the whole trip worthwhile. "The Saint," Reverend Fred called her. She always wore a big smile and shared some homespun talk and a bag of warm cookies. I loved the cookies, but it was the smiles and folksy words of cheer that meant the most.

The years were kinder to me than to the Saint. One day, when I stopped to spend a night with Reverend Fred and his family, he told me the sad news. "The Saint died, Bob. I want you to assist me with the funeral tomorrow."

The next morning, after breakfast, I readied myself for funeral duty. We drove to one of the local funeral homes, and, as was the custom, Reverend Fred and I entered through a rear door. A wall of flowers hid us from the Saint and other family members and mourners who waited for the funeral service to begin.

As the organist played a hymn, Reverend Fred whispered to me, "Do you want to say the prayer or read the obituary?" There was no question about it; I wanted to say the prayer. I'd been caught reading obituaries before. They are usually filled with names of relatives and cities and towns you can't pronounce. So, I always choose praying. Since you love the one you are praying for and the one to whom you're praying, what can go wrong? Plenty.

The music ended and it was my moment to pray. Right on cue I began: "Dear Father in Heaven, I come before You today with a heart filled with love for this dear saint of the church. She has been a pillar of strength all her life, for both the church and her wonderful family gathered here. We are thankful to You for the long years

The Road Scholar

You left her with us. Now she is with You in Heaven and we feel a heavy loss. Her quick smile, her kind words, and her warm cookies were trademarks of her life. Tell her to stand by the gate, and when we make our eternal rounds, we'll stop by for an unending visit. Bless and comfort her family and her friends here today. Amen."

I sat down, feeling the warmth of having shared such a wonderful story with such a great God and all the loving people in the room, although I noticed they shifted uneasily in their chairs. Some cast strange looks in my direction.

As Reverend Fred stood to read the obituary before his sermon, he gave me a look I will not soon forget, and he began: "Leroy Paul Davis was born January 19, 1901, in the town of Parma, Missouri. . . ."

Pastor Fred had failed to tell me his congregation had more than one "Old Saint." The Saint we remembered that day was not a her; it was a him.

Bridge to Andorra

Mile Marker 13,093

Years ago, the niftiest small car in Europe was the Siat, the economical little brother to the well-known Fiat.

I rented a Siat for the drive from Barcelona to Andorra. Andorra is a tiny postage-stamp-sized country a few hundred kilometers north of the Mediterranean Sea, nestled between France and Spain. The route takes you through a few quaint, breathtakingly beautiful Spanish villages.

One village especially impressed me, so I stopped to snap some photos. A bridge in the center of town that crossed a deep gorge caught my attention. Actually, "deep gorge" is an exaggeration; it was more of a sharp crevice between two hills that seemed to stretch for hundreds of yards to its base.

My tiny Siat could go anywhere, so I drove out on the bridge and looked down. There I saw a swift-running river snaking along at the base of the crevice. With half of my body hanging out the car window, I began taking the most exciting photographs any American had ever taken. I wished I had a movie camera or tape recorder to capture the sounds of the rushing waters below.

Then I noticed several townspeople waving at me, and some shouted greetings in their native Spanish. "Someday I really need to learn that language," I thought.

Those Spaniards were such a friendly bunch of people. Their warmth immediately overwhelmed me. I fell in love with them.

My photo mission was done. As I finished my drive across the bridge, I saw and heard the crowd cheering me on. Once safely there, I worried some car or small truck would block my return, so I hurriedly drove back across the bridge to the side where I had started.

A very animated man waving his arms in disgust stopped me and spoke to me in Spanish, and when he realized I was an American, he talked even louder in English telling me I had just driven across a footbridge. "No one has ever dared drive on that bridge before!" he exclaimed. "Don't you understand what a footbridge is?"

Those villagers who had been shouting and waving at me across the bridge wanted this crazy American to get out of their town and go home.

I did.

The Swiss Chickhikers

Mile Marker 17,953

As I drove from Mount Blanc to Geneva one evening, I spotted two people up ahead standing at the edge of the road. They appeared to be hitchhiking. As I came closer, I saw they were both beautiful young women.

As I slowed down, my eyes searched the nearby area for a car. I felt certain they had run out of gas, blew a tire, or had some other malfunction that left them stranded out here alone. But there was no car anywhere, except those driving past us. There were just these two girls, hitchhiking along the highway.

As I neared, they put up their hands. I stopped. They hopped into my car and I drove off.

We rode along a short distance before I realized neither of them had said a word. I'd done all the talking. Feeling embarrassed, I shut up and introduced myself, hoping they would overlook my lack of courtesy and join in the conversation. They just looked at each other and laughed. They didn't understand a single word of English.

Now that is odd: two young, beautiful, non-English-speaking girls alone on a Swiss highway. What's this all about?

I knew I had to find out what they wanted, where their car was, and where I should drop them off.

"Well," I said, "I'm on my way back to Geneva."

"Geneva?" one of them asked.

"Yes, Geneva," I answered to their amazement.

"No, No!" they said. "No Geneva!"

"Turn!" One pointed to a highway sign that indicated an upcoming intersection. "Make turn," she said. I slowed and prepared to turn as she indicated. Once I was off the main highway to Geneva, I felt a little uneasy.

Was I being set up? The three of us rode along for miles in complete silence. When we neared a small Swiss village, both girls were gesturing for me to make another turn.

This time, I was about to lose my temper and just tell them to get out when one pointed to a chalet and said, "Home."

I stopped the car and both girls got out. They came around to the driver's window I had lowered. "Bob, we're sorry. It was just our way of having some fun with a fellow American. We are exchange students from California, and we always wondered what it would be like to act as though we could not communicate. Hope you're not angry with us."

"No," I said, "rescuing two stranded California damsels was not distressing at all."

Sidetracked

Mile Marker 13,336

My many trips to Europe have given me countless pleasurable experiences. I've traveled from the southern coast of Gibraltar to the far northern reaches of Finland, from Portugal in the west to Austria's east boarder.

Nothing tells the tale or gives the true picture of European countries as does travel by train. A train trip somehow brings Europe's beauty to life.

The stations themselves are home to travelers from all over the planet. A master linguist would find them to be a home of enjoyable, cultural, and societal variety. The train passes by quaint villages, picturesque mountains, exotic towns, bustling cities, and desolate plains. In a single day, you experience the nations' majesty, friendliness, warmth, apathy, and distrust.

Even after tens of thousands of miles of crisscrossing the continent by train, my memory goes back to a single night in Germany. I had been on the train all night from the south of France. I felt exhausted from weeks of bone-aching travel, working to fulfill two missions I was assigned.

First, I was to photograph scores of locations for "The High Roads of Europe," my upcoming lecture tour scheduled in Nebraska, North Dakota, and South Dakota. My second job was to see how far I could travel in twenty-one countries of Europe on a European rail pass in sixty days.

By that night in Germany, I had taken more photographs than I would ever need and covered more miles than my numb body deserved.

I looked out the window once again into the thick, black darkness. The gentle swaying of the train and the hypnotic clickety-clack of steel wheels on the tracks added to my drowsiness. It felt as though we stopped a hundred times, but I finally quit counting. With nothing else to do, unable to study the countryside, I yielded to my slumber-laden eyelids and fell asleep.

When I awoke, total darkness surrounded me. The train sat still on the tracks and the engine wasn't running. Even the station lights were black. There was a chill in the air.

I stood and looked out the window, cupping my hands against the glass, trying to focus. There was no station! Questions ran through my mind: Why the silence? Why the chill in the air? And more importantly, where were we? The eeriness of it all was scary.

I threw my only piece of luggage—a single flight bag—over my shoulder and ran to the end of the car. Opening the door, I looked out, searching for some sign of civilization. I saw nothing that represented life.

I stumbled back through the darkness to the other end of the car and looked out the door. Off in the distance, I saw what appeared to be station lights.

I jumped to the ground and made my way toward the lights. I must have walked the distance of a few city blocks or so when everything came into focus. It was the train station, but I didn't have any idea what town or city. For that matter, was I even in Germany? Certainly, I thought, or I would have awakened when the customs officers probed for my passport and travel documents. I remembered none of that.

The world still sat there. My railroad car had been disconnected and pushed to a sidetrack. I slept through it all. Momentarily my life had been derailed. I can't believe the commotion didn't wake me. Furthermore, why didn't the conductor see me and have me change cars to my destination?

Party of One

Mile Marker 12,956

As I walked through the door to the dining room at my favorite motor hotel in Grand Forks, North Dakota, I noticed it sat empty. Probably normal for a midweek afternoon, especially with such dreary weather, I thought. I cast a glance outside to see the gray clouds and cold wind blowing the snow around. Another blizzard had to be on the way.

Often on slow days, I think the waitress or hostess hides out in the kitchen when they should be keeping their eyes open for customers at the door. At least that's how it seemed this time. I stood at the door for what seemed like several minutes. Finally, the server came out of the kitchen, picked up a menu, and walked toward me. "Party of one?" she asked.

I said, "Yes." She led me to a corner table.

Party of one, I repeated in my mind. What is she thinking? When you are alone you are not going to have much of a party. Besides, it isn't my birthday. I'm not wearing a party hat. It is cold as blue blazes outside; there is a chance that a blizzard will blow in any minute. I have nothing to celebrate, so why does Miss Happy Face think I am going to have a party?

I ordered lunch and bided my time thinking about the events of the morning and the upcoming afternoon schedule. Then I noticed three attractive ladies standing in the restaurant doorway. Since the server had disappeared for several minutes, I stood and walked toward the women, picked up three menus, and said to the ladies, "Three for lunch?"

They said yes. I led them to the table right next to mine and seated them. "The server will be with you in a minute," I said, handing each a menu. I sat down at my table less than two feet from theirs.

I eavesdropped on their small talk. Their presence kept me from feeling lonely; I was part of their conversation. Pretty clever move; maybe I'm having a party after all, I thought, with an impish grin on my face. The server didn't know I'd masterminded this little scheme; the ladies didn't know either. I felt great.

I hadn't noticed an elderly couple who had been standing at the restaurant door for quite a while when one of the ladies next to me put her hand on my shoulder and said, "Sir, customers are waiting over there."

I looked up and saw the couple, who could have passed for Maw and Paw Kettle, and said, "Oh, I don't work here."

"You don't work here?" she said. "But, but, you seated us."

"Yes, I did," I said, smiling at her. "I was really lonely, and when I looked up and saw the three of you standing there, I knew if I let the waitress seat you, she'd put you clear across the dining room; my corner of the world would be empty. I didn't want that."

"You could have joined us," she said.

"In my own way, I did. Thanks for brightening my day. I'll treasure these moments for a long, long time," I said.

Springfield Blues

Mile Marker 8,777

My uncle's room was on the third floor of a Springfield, Missouri, hospital. Although I'm not sure why he was there, it really didn't matter. I was on my way from St. Louis to Tulsa, Oklahoma, and decided to stop and visit with him.

After talking with my uncle for a while, a lady dressed in the blue garb of hospital staff came into the room carrying my uncle's lunch.

I was famished and, as I surveyed his tray and caught the sight and aroma of the roast beef, fresh garden peas, and mashed potatoes and gravy, my appetite was aroused like never before.

"Well, I think I'll go down to the cafeteria and get some of that myself," I said.

As I walked into the cafeteria, my empty stomach growled. Everything looked and smelled great. By the time I sat my tray down by the cash register, I had stacked it full of food.

The cashier began to ring up my bill as I pulled out my wallet. There, sticking up out of one of those wallet slots was my ever-popular medical health card. That gave me an idea.

"That'll be $8.45," the cashier said.

I handed her my insurance card and, trying not to smile, waited for her reaction.

"Sorry, sir," she said, "but we can't take this."

"What do you mean you can't take this?" I asked, as though her answer shocked me. "My uncle is on three and he puts his room, medicine, all his meals, and the doctor's bills on his insurance card. Nobody said he couldn't do that. I'm just buying my lunch with mine," I tried to explain.

"Just a minute. I'll talk to the cook," the confused woman said, as she disappeared into the kitchen. Seconds later, she came back with a little guy who was wiping his hands on the tail of his apron.

"Okay, mister, now look," he said in a Brooklyn accent. "You can't do that. I've been with the hospital here for fifteen years, and I've never had this come up before."

I just stood there looking at him, so he went on. "Everyone who comes through the cafeteria line pays for his or her food with cash, a check, or a credit card. Nobody uses their insurance card. So here's what you do." He looked me straight in the eyes and, as seriously as possible, said, "You pay cash for the meal. Okay? Then you eat it. If it makes you sick, check into the hospital, and your next meal is on the card."

By this time, everyone in the cafeteria was staring at us. I felt their sympathy, which made my day. I gobbled the meal down, all the time feeling the eyes of that cashier on my neck, but I never did tell her it was all a joke.

The Gate Crashers

Mile Marker 8,111

The premiere screening of the rushes of a new movie always brings out financial backers, potential funders, celebrities, and special guests. This event was no different, even though it was for a low-budget Christian film. My friend Don and I heard that the rushes would be shown at a 7:00 p.m. banquet. We wanted to be there, too. Unfortunately, we weren't invited, but that didn't stop us from trying to get in.

Rushes—or dailies, as they are often called—are the film footage segments shot during the day or of a particular scene. Often, they are absent sound effects and may include footage that will eventually be eliminated from the film, ending up on the cutting room floor.

Don and I went to the banquet hotel and hung around the lobby, hoping to luck out on tickets or an invitation. No one wanted to give them up.

In the ballroom, we could see workers scurrying around, busily moving tables and chairs, arranging place settings, and putting up decorations. Nearly three hundred people would be attending the dinner, give or take two.

Then we overheard one of the promoters ask the harried hotel clerk if someone could locate a larger projection screen. "Yes," Marilyn said while trying to handle several things at the same time, "we do have one in the properties room. I don't have anyone to get it right now, but I'll take care of it as soon as I can find a couple of people to go bring it up."

Don and I looked at each other. What a break!

As soon as the promoter walked away we approached the hotel staffer. "Hi, Marilyn," I said, looking at her nametag. "We're here to get the screen."

"Oh great," she said, not really looking at us, so busy with details. "Sorry you have to do so much yourself, but we're short a few people here at the hotel, and we're just swamped right now."

"We don't mind," I said, smiling.

"Really," Don added.

We found the properties room and took the screen to the banquet hall. No one bothered us as we put the screen in place. As we adjusted it, the program director came over to compliment us on such fast service. "Now that's the kind of screen I wanted," she said. "It just makes the evening perfect."

So, we had made it into the hall, but we still faced being booted out when the show started.

"You fellows have tickets?" she asked. We shook our heads. "Well, you do now. Some of the invited guests won't make it. Their flights were delayed in Chicago. Can you stay for dinner and the screening?"

"I can," Don said, "How about you, Bob? Can you work it in?"

"Oh, I think I can clear my schedule," I said.

When the dinner and the screening were over, the hostess said she wanted to thank the hotel staff for their excellent service, "especially these two gentlemen who went out of their way to make this event so special. Stand up, guys," she said. We nearly passed out.

Miss America, Jon, and Norris

Mile Marker 7,953

Jon and Norris were both pastors of large churches in the south. They were two of the most resourceful individuals I'd met in quite a while. Norris was a touch more studious and much more inclined to follow the rules than Jon.

The three of us together were mischief waiting to happen.

We had traveled to a convention in Winona Lake, Indiana, held at the Billy Sunday Tabernacle and camp facility. It turned out to be a week I will never forget. We attended classes every day, musical concerts in the afternoon, and a huge rally at night.

The reigning Miss America, attended the events. She drew crowds wherever she went and she always traveled in style. Her promoters chauffeured her around in a new, white luxury convertible. Jon drove a car that was nearly identical. It provided too much temptation for me.

One afternoon, I drove Jon's car to the hotel and picked up Norris to go to lunch. "We" had conceived the perfect plan that featured our pal, Jon.

We spotted Jon holding court with a small group in front of the coffee shop on the town's main street. This was our chance to execute "our" plan.

Norris got into the trunk of the car. I was supposed to drive up to where Jon stood and push the automatic trunk lid release, and Norris would jump out, yelling, "Surprise!" Norris and I knew this would be an embarrassment to Jon.

As soon as Norris settled down in the trunk, I turned the radio on and shifted the sound to the rear speaker. Norris couldn't hear what I would say to Jon.

When I pulled up to the curb where Jon stood, I waved at him to get into the car. Then, in a whisper, I told him about Norris being in the trunk. Then I told him the rest of the story.

We drove to the hotel where Miss America stayed, stopping in front of the entrance. I turned down the radio and asked Norris if he was ready. I heard a muffled yes come from the trunk.

I pushed the release button and the trunk flew open with Norris right behind it.

"SURPRISE!" he yelled, in his strongest preacher's voice. There stood two hundred or so people milling around hoping to get a glimpse of Miss America.

Jon and I burst out with laughter. Our plan was accomplished perfectly. Norris slinked away red-faced.

Sudden Death

Mile Marker 1,247

Many people really can't appreciate what driving was like before interstate highways. Those days were really "special" for those of us who traveled the country regularly. We learned that during construction season, you could never be sure you could get there from here. Long trips often became epic journeys, or so it seemed.

My friends Clenton and Glenn were on a tight schedule to meet up with me in Chicago. The three of us were to make a presentation at a convention, and they had the projector, film, and related visuals for the event, so there was no way I could just wing it. If they didn't show up on time, I would be devastated.

The guys had been driving the old highways for hours when nature and an empty gas tank forced them into a wee-hour-of-the-morning pit stop. After paying the attendant, Glenn pulled the car to the edge of the parking lot and stopped to shut his eyes for a few seconds. Clent curled up in the backseat to do the same.

The car sat facing a huge billboard advertising the gas station. Glenn opened his window slightly to let fresh air in, leaving the engine running to keep the heat coming. The headlights illuminated the billboard.

Glenn fell sound asleep. So did Clent.

Suddenly, Glenn's foot slipped off the brake pedal and onto the accelerator. The engine roared and the noise startled Glenn awake, his eyes immediately focusing on the brightly lit billboard straight ahead. Instinct engaged as he slammed his foot on the brake pedal.

When he didn't feel the car screech to a stop, he screamed, "We're going to die!"

Glenn's scream startled Clenton awake, who then smashed his head on the car's ceiling as he scrambled to get to his feet. "Do you think I should drive for a while?" Clent asked.

There was no danger. The car was still in park.

Ricochet

Mile Marker 8,997

Golf is a great pastime for millions of Americans, and as a result, I am sure ball-makers are all millionaires. Zillions of golf balls lay in the long grass and among the trees. If they could, I think they would laugh aloud at the frustrated golfers walking within inches of them, never making their discovery.

Then there is the question of what happens to the old and scarred golf balls. I am convinced golfers save them, eventually paint them fluorescent colors, and open a miniature golf course. These miniature golf courses attract guys like me who have nothing better to do and wouldn't be caught dead walking a regulation eighteen-hole course on a hot day.

Glenn and I stopped at a miniature golf course for nine holes during a trip to Evansville, Indiana. It started out fun, because the first hole is always just a flat, felt-carpeted green, with a slight turn to the right or left. You almost always get a two, ready to take on the rest of the course.

Eventually, though, you come face to face with the infamous windmill—hole number nine. The evil course-designer made it so you had to tap the ball up a ramp at a precise speed so it would coast down the other side. There, it had to miss the moving windmill blades and fall into the mouth of the tube that aims the ball at the cup. It was impossible.

Before Glenn even got the ball up the ramp, he was way past par. Each time he hit the ball, it would nearly reach the top, stop for what seemed like minutes, and then roll back down. Or he'd give it a good pop, and it would jump the ledge and end up in the grass.

He put the ball on the tee once again. I had already lost count and he gave up caring.

He meant to win this battle no matter what; he'd succeed or die trying. He put everything he had into this swing, connecting with the ball and sending it flying toward the next county. He would have succeeded, too, except for the brick wall of the windmill.

The ball ricocheted off the wall right back at Glenn, smacking him squarely in the noggin. He had scored a hole in one . . . forehead. He lay knocked-out cold. I knelt beside him and prayed. I was afraid he was seriously injured. When he came around, we decided to forget another round of golf and headed for the nearest refreshment stand.

No Tanks, I'm Full

Mile Marker 5,556

The gas station sat on a knoll just off the main highway. We pulled into the dirt driveway and felt the thump of tires bouncing in and out of potholes. We laughed, thinking somewhere in the midst of these potholes lay a driveway.

Those potholes became like tiny ponds every time it rained.

In those days, a gas station attendant pumped the gas while providing a number of small services for drivers—checking the oil, washing the windows, and airing the tires.

I drove up and parked behind an old Ford. The attendant had stuck the gasoline nozzle in the Ford's filler pipe, and the volatile liquid flowed freely down into the tank. The handle had one of those newfangled automatic devices on it that shut off when the gas tank got full. I never have understood how that works. It's just as well, because back then it didn't work half the time. This was one of those times.

The Ford was full, but the gas kept coming. The attendant lay half under the Ford's hood, checking the oil. From our vantage point, all we could see were his legs sticking out. He never saw the gasoline gushing out onto the ground. It began forming little puddles in the nearest pothole.

Clenton laughed hysterically, oblivious to the potential life-threatening explosion. I tried to shout to the attendant, but words wouldn't come out of my mouth.

The gauge on the pump spun quickly as the gas flowed. We felt sure the gauge read at least thirty gallons, an outrageous amount for that little Ford.

Finally finished with checking the oil, the attendant climbed out from under the hood, slammed it down, and, while wiping his hands on a dirty rag, looked at the pump, then at the driver, and back at the pump.

"I'll just round it off to five dollars," he said. The driver looked at the attendant, then at the pump, and back at the attendant. Without saying a word, he handed him five dollars, grinned, and drove away.

"Fill 'er up?" the attendant said as he walked nonchalantly up to my car.

"Um. How far is it to Chicago?" I asked, having decided that in no way would I buy gas from this guy.

"Two hundred forty miles," he said, looking off down the highway.

"Thank you," I said as I drove away, trying to avoid the pothole overflowing with gasoline.

"Two hundred forty miles, huh?" Clent said as we hit the highway again. "That means it can't be more than eighty-five."

The Cat Got My Tongue

Mile Marker 3,340

I saw the word "Information" hanging above a desk in the train lobby and was excited that at least some German words were almost exactly the same as their English counterpart. I had just arrived at the Munich train station, and seeing that booth brought relief. The knowledgeable attendant standing there would have all the information I would need. I knew with her help I would make it to my Vienna, Austria, rally on time. I needed to know the track and the boarding time for the train to Vienna.

I also wanted to avoid being embarrassed . . . again. Since I didn't speak German or any other language in vogue at the time, I decided to use good old American ingenuity. I'll say "Vienna," point to the trains, and shrug my shoulders. That certainly should work, I figured. It had before.

"Sprechen Sie Deutsch?" the blonde girl behind the information counter asked. I shook my head.

"Parlez-vous français?" I shook my head.

"Italiano?" I shook my head again and smiled.

I had a backup plan, so I laid my European rail pass map on the counter, pointed to Munich, and then to Vienna.

"Do you speak English, sir?" she asked in perfect English.

"Yes, ma'am."

"Well, sir, your train leaves in three minutes on track seven, and I don't know why you put us both through all this."

"Um, danke," I said, and quietly left her wicket.

"Der nächste bitte?" I heard as I walked away, once again thinking, I really need to learn this language.

A Voice from Above

Mile Marker 839

The day had been hectic. I had taken on too many campaigns at one time, and all of them were going full swing. It seemed as though I had to make a decision every second. I felt the pressure and wished for relief, but in the campaign business, sometimes you don't even have time for a bathroom break.

As the evening wore on, I wore out. All I wanted was to get back to my rented room and go to sleep.

Mercifully, the workday finally ended and I drove home, surrounded by peace and quiet. Being alone at times like these always felt good. It gave me time to reflect on the events of the day, think about tomorrow, and plan for other events days ahead.

To save money during those early years, I would rent a room in a private home instead of staying in an expensive hotel or motel. I looked for a place in the area where my candidate campaigned. It helped me get better acquainted with the people of the district and talk with them about the local issues. That was really important.

Mine was more like a tourist home with one exception: My quarters were in the basement. Before going to bed that night, I quietly crept up the stairs to the first floor to use the restroom. The house sat enveloped in darkness and utter quietness. The family who lived there were church folks who were early to bed, early to rise.

I closed the door to the bathroom and stood there in the dark. Suddenly, I heard God speaking. Well, at least, I heard the word of the Lord coming from up above.

I froze for a second trying to get a sense of what was going on. Then I remembered; the man of the house listened to the Bible on cassette tape every night. He had left the bathroom speaker turned on.

Since I had to do laundry the next morning anyway, washing out my freshly soiled shorts wouldn't make any difference.

(And no, the passage wasn't from the book of John.)

Okay to Swim

Mile Marker 11,353

Everyone loved Andy Allen just because he was a great guy. Back then, people everywhere recognized him as one of the popular tent evangelists of the day.

He handled the scriptures with depth and breadth and handled his weight about the same; he was as tall as he was wide. Andy weighed 356 pounds. He often talked to me about his weight and wanted to shed pounds, but couldn't.

Andy felt somewhat self-conscious about his obesity, but it never made him hide from people or curtail his voracious eating habits.

One day, during a series of revival meetings in Oklahoma City, back before hotel and motel swimming pools became popular, Andy said, "Today I'm going swimming, and you should go with me."

Did I mention I weighed 106 pounds then or that I felt very self-conscience about it? (A note about being underweight: You have no idea the remarks people make about you "Look, you can read a newspaper through him"; "He's so skinny the wind could blow him away"; or "Are you sickly?")

Just the thought of people staring at me made me want to run and hide, which I sometimes did. So there was no way I was going to put myself through an embarrassing journey to a city swimming pool. It was out of the question.

"But Bob, it's so hot," the persuasive preacher reminded me. Finally, I gave in and said I'd go.

I didn't even own a pair of swimming trunks. He dropped me off at a men's clothing store on the way and I found a pair that actually fit me.

When we arrived at the pool, I saw that almost everyone else in town had the same idea. They were all here trying to cool off.

We located the changing room, and minutes later, I walked out into the sun's glare and the crowd's stare. Andy had squeezed his 356 pounds into a massive pair of swim trunks and trailed behind me to the pool's edge. Each inch of my 106-pound frame was exposed to the world.

As if in unison, the crowd went silent. Hundreds of eyes turned toward us. Their scorching glare felt hotter than the sun.

Long before my feet hit the pool, I hit the changing room.

Muffle It, Lady

Mile Marker 9,966

The "lady" ahead of me drove erratically. She sped up, slowed down, and then zigzagged back and forth across the road. I put up with this nonsense for a couple of miles, and as soon as I could, I passed her.

It felt great to be making good time again, until I pulled nearer to the next car, driven by a guy this time. He must have taken driver's training at the same school she did.

Then it happened. The muffler fell off his car. Thankfully, he was just far enough ahead of me so I could make a maneuver and straddle the muffler as it swirled across the road. The lady fared more poorly, as she was following so closely behind me. She hit the muffler, and I could see right away it made her madder than a wet hen.

She must have thought the muffler came off my car, because she took off after me like a cop chasing down a thief. When I turned south, she turned south. The faster I drove, the faster she drove.

Finally, I got a mile ahead of her and quickly turned onto another highway. I saw a bowling alley a short distance down the road and zipped into the parking lot, immediately driving around back to hide.

It worked.

I peeked around the corner of the building and searched the horizon. She was nowhere in sight.

Finally, I drove back to the highway and headed for my next stop. There she stood—with the cops. They flagged me down, and she proceeded to tell them I'd almost wrecked her car when my muffler flew off and hit her car.

"But officer, look for yourself," I pleaded, pointing to the underside of my car. One of the officers took a quick look and then told me to go on my way.

I could still hear her raging rant as I drove away. Soon, though, her voice became increasingly muffled.

A Rack of Bones

Mile Marker 8,009

My earlier days of speaking at rallies, conventions, and other gatherings of young people were some of the greatest times of my life. I even found ways to use my skinny body as a source of humor. With such a body, you had to have a sense of humor about it or go hide in a closet.

The rally director in Pocahontas, Arkansas, was about as overweight as anyone can get. No one wondered how he stayed so portly. It was obvious to all who knew him well. He delighted in early morning, noon, afternoon, evening, and late night feasts.

He especially enjoyed homemade cornbread crumbled in clabber, which is a thick and lumpy sour milk that, in my opinion, should be thrown to the hogs—except hog farmers probably think better of it.

For some people, all they long for are the simple things of life: food, family, and friends. Waking up to the aroma of an early morning Arkansas breakfast is enough to make you abandon your diet and throw caution to the wind. The smell of a fresh batch of homemade buttermilk biscuits, right out of the oven, mingled with a whiff of frying bacon, almost trumps the scent of coffee perking on the kitchen counter.

One late night as he gorged on cornbread and clabber, he looked up at me and said, "Bob, you'll never die."

"What do you mean I'll never die?" I asked as I sipped my black coffee.

"Well, there are only two diseases that could kill you: skin disease or bone disease." He chuckled at his own joke with his enormous frame shaking in the chair. By now, he was roaring with laughter, which was not a pretty sight.

There was something contagious about his laughter. I joined in, and my participation only added fuel to the fire. His hilarity induced a variety of guttural sounds, snorting, and finally a flood of tears. As the laughter subsided, I found my voice and said, "You're the one who will never die. There's only one disease that'll silence your beating heart."

"What's that?" he said.

Staring at the double set of tires around his middle, I said, "Stomach trouble."

My remark triggered another round of laughter. I couldn't help but love and appreciate his pedestrian sense of humor.

Speechless

Mile Marker 9,805

I attended Bible school in St. Louis, Missouri. To help with the expenses, I got a job downtown at a shoe manufacturing company.

While their major products were shoes, they also had a subsidiary that designed and custom made baseball gloves for professional athletes, as well as manufactured a variety of related sports equipment.

The streetcar was my means of transportation from the school dorm three miles north to my place of employment. Every morning I caught the Jefferson streetcar and entertained myself listening to the monotonous clicking of the steel wheels on the tracks or studying the faces of the assortment of business people, office workers, and laborers who also road this car. I sometimes wondered what their lives were like. Were they in transition or stuck in a rut with work, home, and too little free time? My brother often said a rut is just a grave with both ends knocked out.

Some of the passengers were easy to read; written on their faces were the cares of yesterday, the challenges of today, and a paltry few hopes for tomorrow.

When my shift was over at the shoe factory, I allowed the few who rushed out to catch the next southbound to push ahead. Often, until the crowds dissipated, I would walk a short distance down the street and enjoy the window displays that were such an attraction in St. Louis. There was real artistry in these displays. They were not just mannequins wearing the latest fashions. The office stores, hardware stores, and sporting goods businesses went all out to lure customers into their places; their only chance with the hundreds of passersby was to have a "hook" in their windows to draw them in. Most of them did.

Along with the department stores were renowned restaurants, a cluster of well-known hotels, and, of course, the famous hub of human culture and home of the homeless: Union Station. With its boutiques, shoeshine stands, and the unforgettable Fred Harvey's—my all-time favorite for coffee, food, and people watching—you couldn't spend time at a more enjoyable haunt.

It was getting late. I had to get back to the dorm for dinner, so I hurried to the streetcar stop and waited for the southbound, when a placard vendor approached me.

Even though I had a job, I was nearly broke. Often to save money, I would walk the three miles back to the dorm. By the time I paid tuition, bought tokens for the streetcar, and took care of my laundry, I sure didn't have money left for this guy's placards, so I tried to ignore him. He would not be ignored. He launched into his canned sales pitch asking me to buy one of his thirty-five-cent, blue wall mottos with glittery lettering that read "Home Sweet Home" or one of a dozen other slogans.

I looked at him and used both hands in a flurry of gestures, with my arms flailing in the air and an occasional thump to my chest, faking sign language; he got the message. I thought he would now just give up and walk away.

He didn't.

Instead, he quickly put his bundle of mottos between his knees and held up both hands. Oh no! I thought. This guy really knows sign language. But he didn't. Now with his hands free, he used his fingers to flash a three and a five—thirty-five.

As an answer to a prayer or maybe dumb luck, the streetcar rumbled up just then. I jumped on board thinking, *He needs a motto that says "35 CENTS EACH."*

My Mic and Dean

Mile Marker 10,222

He was the thirty-seventh person to occupy the position of the United States Secretary of State executing our foreign policy, and I was impressed with him. From the very beginning, I appreciated his down-to-earth approach and his common sense. I have followed the career of Dean Rusk ever since the first time we met. During the 1960s, I had a chance to hear him speak in person at a large gathering. On that particular day, he keynoted the annual convention of the International Platform Association at the famed Shoreham Hotel in Washington, DC, I hurried down to the ballroom to get a seat as close to the platform as possible.

I walked into the convention auditorium and saw that a large crowd had already gathered. The emcee introduced Rusk as I searched the room for a seat. I certainly didn't want to stand in the back of the room. As I walked up the side aisle toward the front, I continued to search for an empty seat. No such luck.

I did, however, spot a large, heavy, black, wooden box sitting open along the wall. It contained several microphones, cables, and other related broadcast paraphernalia. Obviously, it belonged to a radio or television broadcast network that was covering the event.

In those days, security was relatively lax, so no one paid attention to me. Certain that everyone was focused on Rusk at the podium, I walked up to the box and picked up a microphone. I took an envelope out of my inside coat pocket and held the mic close to my lips, pretending to read softly, like an announcer at a golf tournament.

As Rusk spoke, I frequently whispered into the microphone.

At the end of his speech, I rushed toward him and, sticking my mic near his mouth, conducted my "interview." Once done, I calmly walked back to the box and set the microphone back inside.

Quickly, I went to a telephone to tell anyone who would listen about my private conversation with Secretary of State Dean Rusk—just Mic, Dean, and me. What a day!

Hanky-Panky

Mile Marker 11422

Leroy Hanky was about the funniest preacher I've ever met. He was the pastor of a church near Cape Girardeau, Missouri. Hanky had a homespun way about him, one of those guys who you are never quite sure if he is serious or teasing—and as often as not, "he'd be a joshin' ya."

I appeared for a series of meetings in southern Illinois, not far from The Cape, as folks down there call it. One day, in walked Leroy Hanky. He sat down in the audience and joined in song and worship with the congregation just like he was at home. I learned later that everywhere Leroy Hanky went was home.

After the service, he walked up and introduced himself. "Pastor Leroy Panky," he said, shoving his hand out at me. "Me an' the wife wanta take you out for somethin' ta eat. Have ya et, yet?"

"No, not yet," I said, already intrigued by this plain-speakin' gent.

He told me he was the pastor of a small congregation near The Cape. During the next two weeks, he'd stop by often and say, "Come on, Bobby. We'll go get a Coney dog and a coffee drink."

"Sometime this eve'nin'," he'd say, which I found out could be any time of the day, "we're gonna bus' a watermelon." I love watermelon and the unbelievable mess you make trying to eat it.

A friend of mine visited Leroy Hanky at his church one evening. "Brother Fred," Pastor Leroy said in his usual manner of mispronouncing important words in the English language, "you come on up on the flatform and sit a spell." Fred felt honored.

During the congregational singing, Leroy leaned over to Fred and said, "We done run out of seatin' compassion, so we're buildin' a condition on the back. Be finished come spring!"

The next time I see Leroy and Fred, I know they'll both have stories to tell. I can hardly wait.

Alone in the Dark

Mile Marker 10,315

I always took a mug of coffee with me into the darkroom. As I processed film and printed glossies, it felt good to enjoy sipping on a fresh hot cup of java.

I'd make a print and then reach up to the shelf for my coffee. I'd take a sip, print another picture, and then repeat the process. By the time all the prints had been made and hung on the line to dry, my coffee cup was dry, too. I had usually consumed a couple of mugs of coffee. The time just passed better that way.

Many nights in a row, I went into that photo lab to process the new batch of photographs. Every day presents a new challenge for those of us involved in political campaigns. It is important to spin a new pictorial story, so to speak, to draw voters into your candidate's web. Nothing shows the candidate's involvement in the community like photographs of him or her working with people, helping solve problems, speaking to various groups, and attending important neighborhood meetings. Capturing the candidate in action lets the voters see interest, respect, and commitment from this would-be officeholder.

On one night, as I entered the darkroom, I didn't notice the half-finished mug of coffee I had left there the night before. Needless to say, it had turned wretchedly stale and cold. I sat my fresh mug of coffee beside it.

A few prints later, I reached for my coffee and picked up the cold mug by mistake. When I took a drink, I felt something sticking to my upper lip. I wiped my mouth with the back of my hand and examined it closely under the darkroom's red light. It was a dead spider that I instinctively threw on the floor and smashed with my foot, thinking he won't have the guts to do that again.

You can picture me caught in that web of horror!

Hamming It Up in Spain

Mile Marker 9,148

Understanding the religious customs of various cultures is critical when you travel abroad. In fact, lack of understanding will create its own embarrassments—maybe even dangers.

I learned this one day as I drove north in Spain, a few hundred kilometers from Barcelona and the Mediterranean coast. My drive to this tiny village took me through some of the most beautiful and historical spots in the country.

Hungry for lunch, I stopped at a small grocery store to buy some fruit and bottled water. Once inside, I noticed they also had a meat and poultry counter—the sliced ham looked especially delicious.

I picked out some fruit and a bottle of water and asked the clerk to cut a couple slices of ham. I looked forward to a real luncheon feast.

Then I picked up the bread. The owner instantly got angry with me. I resented his attitude and became more confused when he refused to let me buy the bread. After all, this fresh loaf of bread would make my meal complete.

I had no idea that the bread I grabbed was a special loaf, sacred to him and the people of his faith. For them, using it as sandwich material with ham was a sacrilege. Later, friends told me I was lucky he sold me anything, given my affront to his faith.

This taught me a valuable lesson: We must understand the customs and beliefs of the people of the lands we are visiting and be sensitive to them.

My personal mission on this trip to Europe was to learn about the people in select countries. This episode gave me a new hunger in my quest, to have a better understanding of the culture before being such a ham.

The Scout Leader's Pick-Up

Mile Marker 9,050

Mr. Bradly loved children and they loved him. Though an adult, he had a child's heart. Sometimes his youthful nature exposed a certain naivety, but that just added to his joyful character.

Early on in life, he decided to be an elementary school teacher. Outside of the normal school day, he tutored children who were having difficulty in school. Bradly (for some strange reason, teachers call each other by their last name) volunteered to work at camp, and he especially enjoyed scouting activities.

We both taught at the same school in the inner-city of one of the most violent towns in America. The FBI listed this as the most violent city in the nation three years in a row. With that distinction, teachers paid close attention to each other and walked to their cars at the end of the day in teams.

On one scouting day, Bradly proudly wore his uniform to school. Seeing this scout interact with students and other adults made a positive impression on the children.

That day, he chose to drive to a nearby hotel for lunch. On the way, he noticed a woman standing on the corner in the pouring rain. Always the helpful scout, he thought she might be one of his students' mothers, and so, he stopped to give her a ride.

"How far are you going?" she asked.

"I can take you as far as the hotel. I'll be stopping there," he answered.

"That's great," she said. "I haven't been there in a long, long time." She looked at him and added, "Will you be able to bring me back, too?"

"I sure will," he said. "This is your lucky day. I will take you down to the hotel and bring you back."

"It looks like it's a lucky day for both of us," she said. As Bradly pulled into the hotel parking lot, she said, "Just let me out here and I'll wait for you on the inside."

"Well, I'm going to have a quick lunch before I go back."

"A quick lunch? What do you mean?" She looked at him and shook her head in wonderment. "I'm on the clock here, mister. I don't have time for you to have lunch and take care of our business, too."

"Business? What business?" the confused scout leader asked, absolutely clueless.

"Look, boy scout, you picked me up on my corner and promised to take me to the hotel, and now you say you're going to have lunch first." By now, she had her hands on her hips and became downright indignant. "No way. I'm a mile or more from my corner, and you're not just going to dump me off here in the rain."

Finally, when he got back to school, he told all of us about the rude lady he picked up and drove to the hotel. Bradly's eyebrows raised and cheeks turned slightly red as the teachers explained to him just who and what he had hooked up with.

Winning by a Nose

Mile Marker 6,705

City Councilman John had served with distinction for several years. His re-election, under normal circumstances, would be a cinch. Then redistricting happened and the campaign became complicated.

The city's population had grown and district lines were redrawn, creating new political boundaries, John ended up in the same district as his good friend Dick, another incumbent councilman. Instead of a shoo-in campaign, John had to burn shoe leather just to hope for survival.

As the campaign wore on, John and Dick gained equal voter support. John was worried the race might end in his defeat.

"Bob, we have to do something," John said to me. "If things go on the way they are now, I may lose this election, and I don't want that to happen. Besides, Dick's not as qualified as I am."

"Okay, I like that attitude, but how do we tell the voters?" I asked.

His answer was simple: "You tell the truth about him. He gave special favors to his family and hired his wife to work in his office. Use that in our new literature."

"How do you know these things, and are they a matter of record?" I asked.

"They are true. He's the one who violated the public trust, and the only fair thing to do is let the residents know how their tax dollars are being spent," John said.

I drafted a four-page tabloid that featured the story about the "family matter" and showed it to John. "That's what I want to do," he said, as he carefully inspected it.

I wanted to make sure John was courageous enough to put his opponent on the spot, so I added, "It's a little strong, but by exposing this story, it will show the voters you two are really two different people with different values. This piece will raise a fury and you may not win, but if you are comfortable with it, let's go with it."

He was and we did.

When the tabloid hit the streets a few days later, Dick got a copy of it and came looking for John. Spotting him, Dick got out of his car and walked up to John and punched him in the nose and then shoved him to the ground.

Before going to the hospital, John drove to my office to show me the damage. "Well, I just lost the election," he said, dejectedly. "When this story hits the newspaper, the voters will turn on me."

The story made front-page news the next day, and the election was over.

John won by a nose.

The Rainbow

Mile Marker 10,401

It rained steadily all night during my stay in Philadelphia and continued until early morning. I needed to drive to a nearby hotel to meet a candidate, and so I began the trek.

As I drove, I spotted a beautiful rainbow hanging across the breadth of the sky; it seemed to stretch across the entire state. What a wonder. God gives us these exciting reminders of His promise and presence. It was so brilliant, I could hardly take my eyes off it.

I drove down the clean, wet highway enjoying the aroma of fresh, rain-cleansed air. At the hotel, I went into the dining room where I would meet the candidate. I arrived a few minutes early.

Across from me sat two ladies. They talked about their drive that morning and how much they liked the gentle rain. I enjoyed eavesdropping on their conversation. This is a common pastime of mine, listening to the human drama of two friends talking about their experiences. It connects me to the world and to people; it sure beats being alone.

I gathered from what they said that they, too, had spent the night near Philadelphia. They were headed to Washington, DC, and had stopped for breakfast.

One of the ladies got up and went to the restroom. "What a beautiful morning," I said to the other. "I couldn't help but marvel at the sight of the colorful rainbow that seemed to stretch across the entire sky. Did you folks see it?"

"Well, I didn't notice it myself. I'm sure it was a great sight to see," she replied. "I'm sure my sister saw it; she was driving."

"Well, I don't see how you could have missed it; it was absolutely stunning. You must have not been awake yet," I teased. She didn't respond.

When her sister returned and took her seat, the seeing-eye dog lying beneath the table shifted his position. I was horrified. The rainbow of reds and pinks that flooded across my face and the rush of embarrassment that engulfed me made a very bold statement: How could I have missed her dog? How stupid of me. I must not have been awake yet!

A Left Hooker

Mile Marker 14,237

Political conventions usually are a lot of fun, at least for people like me. I attend every year, if I can, and take in all the events. I make a point of seeing all the political candidates and listening to most of the convention speakers, especially the keynote address.

I prefer being an alternate rather than a regular delegate. As an alternate, I can still freely roam the floor and attend all the hospitality rooms and private gatherings, but others actually do the convention business—debating rules, proposing resolutions, and making endorsements.

Convention organizers assign delegates red ribbons, while alternates wear blue ribbons. These are attached to the identification cards we all wear on our lapels. It makes it easy for organizers to see who is authorized to be on the convention floor and engage in the convention wheeling and dealing. A lot of business is done at conventions; it's not all politics.

As this day and evening wore on, I became extremely tired and could not wait for the final gavel of the night. I felt near exhaustion by the time I walked into the hotel coffee shop for a light snack before going up to my room.

I went right to the counter, hoping not to run into anyone I knew so I could avoid a long conversation. I got lucky. I got the last empty stool. Then I placed my order.

"So, what do you do around here for entertainment?" asked the woman next to me. I noticed she wore a red ribbon and nametag. I didn't want to be rude, but neither did I want to get into a long discourse.

"Well, I'm going to go up to bed," I said.

"That sounds interesting," she responded immediately.

"It really does, especially after the kind of day we've had," I said.

She quickly said, "I'd like to go up with you, and will for fifty dollars."

I was stunned. Where did this remark come from? She's a convention delegate and, unless she's joking around, should keep this kind of talk to herself. Hoping to put an end to her proposal, I said in a loud voice, "Fifty dollars? I usually get seventy-five or a hundred!"

"You get seventy-five!" she said, taken aback. "I'm talking about you paying me!"

"No way, Jose!" I said, smiling at her.

It was then that I noticed her nametag and red ribbon didn't really look like the tag I wore or those worn by convention delegates, alternate delegates, staff, or platform guests.

This "conventioneer" had a different assignment. I figured some people probably bought her hook(er), line, and sinker.

A Snake in the Woodpile

Mile Marker 4,906

Appearing before audiences in Alabama offers special rewards. The people are among the friendliest in the nation, and they know how to cook and eat, which makes them great entertainers. I never passed up a chance to visit there.

Besides its great citizens, Alabama has many other wonderful features. I remember the red clay, fabulous cities, great monuments, and rich history. Hardworking Alabamans provide America with some really great products. Huntsville houses a huge missile complex, and its world famous missile program launched the United States' claim as number one in space exploration.

On one such trip to rural Alabama, a volunteer group planned to do yard work at the park on Saturday. I had free time, so I said I would help. "What time do we start?"

"Be here at 8:00 a.m. sharp, and we'll have coffee and donuts before we begin," the director said, quickly accepting my offer.

That Saturday morning as we got started, he handed me a pair of leather gloves. "No, I won't need them," I said, trying to sound macho.

We began working, piling short pieces of logs on a pickup truck. This was really simple and easy work, and I felt good helping with a community project. After several minutes, he asked, "Are you really sure you don't want these gloves? I never do this kind of work without a good pair of thick leather gloves."

"Nope, I'm okay," I said.

"Well, suit yourself. But I'm afraid of rattlesnakes myself. I got bit by one right here in this yard, and it took a long time to get over it."

I grabbed the gloves, put them on, and tried to figure out how to cut the work assignment short. If there's one thing that really rattles me, it's working around snakes.

The Blind Driver

Mile Marker 5,757

As Glenn and I drove across Missouri, we decided it was time to stop for gas and stretch our weary legs. We looked for a station that had an adjoining coffee shop so we could use the restroom and freshen up as well.

In those days, you could leave the car in the care of the station attendant, who would gas it up, put air in the tires, check the oil, and wash the windows. This left us free to go inside and enjoy a leisurely cup of coffee or two.

Glenn is just four years older than me but has had gray hair since he was a teenager. People often thought he was my father. He certainly shares my strange sense of humor.

On this day, we found a tiny gas station with a relatively clean-looking café attached. I pulled up to the pump. "Fill it up," I told the attendant. "My dad and I are going in to get a cup of coffee."

"Right," Glenn grunted and grinned. He sat in the passenger seat.

I looked over at Glenn and noticed he had his sunglasses on. It struck me he looked every bit like an old blind man. "Glenn, sit there and I'll come and help you out of the car. Let's have some fun."

As I opened his door and took his arm, Glenn fell right into the role. He stumbled once or twice on the way into the restaurant and awkwardly straddled the stool at the counter. I thought spilling his coffee was a little over the top, but it played well to the small crowd of people who were dipping their donuts into steaming hot coffee.

I paid for our coffee and gas and led Glenn out the door. "Take me to the driver's seat," Glenn whispered. A smile broke across my face.

He climbed into the car as I rushed around to get in on the passenger side. He started the engine and put the car in gear. Dust and gravel were kicked up behind us as we roared out of the gas station and onto the highway.

As we drove away, I looked back over my shoulder at the small crowd that had gathered in front of the coffee shop. I doubled up in laughter as I saw their mouths gaped open in either fear or amazement—or both.

Glenn didn't have to weave down the highway to drive home his sense of humor, but he did anyway.

The Wasp Attack

Mile Marker 397

The hot sun beat down on the pavement and radiated into the car. Ted had been driving for several hours and wanted to stop at an air-conditioned coffee shop to cool off. Those days, cars seldom had air-conditioning, so cross-country traveling on hot days like this one were miserable.

Ted slowed as he entered a small town, and as he did, a wasp flew in the window, buzzing across his line of vision. He tried to brush the creature out of the car but was unsuccessful. The wasp flew past his face a couple of times, and Ted swatted it in an attempt to kill it. That failed, too. Then it disappeared, but he felt sure it still lingered somewhere in the car.

Frustrated, he grabbed a magazine lying on the front seat, rolled it tight, and waited. He planned his attack for the next time the wasp flew past. He hoped it would land on either the dashboard or the windshield where he would have a clear shot.

He remembered reading about the fly that accompanied Charles Lindberg on his trans-Atlantic flight and wondered if it was as annoying as this little guy was. Ted thought flies, of course, don't sting like wasps do, so he needed to kill it or knock it out the window as soon as possible.

His luck suddenly changed . . . sort of. The wasp roared into high gear and flew straight at his face. Ted tightly clutched his trusty magazine and wildly swatted at the beast, knocking him out the window. The wasp's hastened flight barely preceded Ted's sunglasses that had been caught by the magazine's glancing blow. That force flung them out the window.

Ted watched helplessly as the glasses landed in oncoming traffic and the wheels of a pickup truck smashed them. He avoided the wasp sure enough but felt stung by the loss of his sunglasses.

Sock It to You

Mile Marker 427

Driving through rural roads in the south sometimes seems like visiting a mobile shopping mall. Makeshift stands sit alongside the highway, where people sell everything from homegrown fruits and vegetables, to handmade quilts, to knickknacks, crafts, and antiques. My favorites were the roadside barbecue stands in the Carolinas.

My friends Harvey and Graham were on their way to a town in southern Alabama where they planned to attend an auction. On their way, they spotted something new to them: a man selling socks. The hood and trunk of his car were piled high with bundles of them, all neatly tied together. A hand-lettered sign read: 12 dozen pairs of sox $3.

"Wouldn't that be 144 socks for three dollars?" Harvey said, looking at Graham. "Am I right here?"

"Probably, but I think it would total 144 pairs, or 288 socks," Graham said.

"It doesn't make sense he could sell socks for that price. By golly, I think we should stop and buy some. It's worth it," Graham added.

"What say we buy a couple of bundles each?" Harvey said, really taken by the fantastic bargain lying in front of his eyes.

"Sounds good to me," Graham replied.

Harvey couldn't brake the car fast enough. They were amazed as they searched through the huge piles of socks.

"Look, he's got socks of every color and size," Graham said. "I think I'll buy some for the kids and maybe even buy some to give to a church or charity to help poor folks."

They each bought three bundles and celebrated their good fortune as they drove the rest of the way to the auction.

Late that evening in their motel room, they untied the bundles of socks and began to spread them out on the two king-size beds in their room. They put all the white socks in a pile on one of the beds and all the colored socks on the other bed. They began sorting the white socks.

They each had 864 socks to sort; matching them up took much longer than they thought it would. By the wee hours of the morning, they came to the conclusion that although they had 1,728 socks altogether, they didn't have a single pair that matched.

"No wonder it was such a good deal, Harvey," a weary Graham said, throwing a handful back onto the pile.

"The man that sold us these things is probably long gone. If he's still there when we go home, I want to stop and sock him," Harvey said.

Good Golly, Miss Molly

Mile Marker 4,524

Kay had two cats. One was old and sickly and had to be put down, but that is another story. The tender care she gave her cats and two dogs all their lives evidenced her love for animals.

Now that Kay was moving to a nearby town, she had her hands full with all the details of packing, ordering the moving van, and coordinating the volunteer help of family and friends. She wanted to get settled before she brought her animals home, so she boarded the two dogs at a kennel and left the cats for me to bring on my last trip.

Molly was shy and had never been friendly toward me. I arrived at Kay's old house with the cat carrier in hand, ready to fetch Molly, but Molly didn't want to be fetched.

The tri-level home had three bedrooms and a bath on the upper floor. It was there that Molly holed up. I closed all the doors except for her room and went in to shoo her out. Sitting on the top shelf of the closet, she leaped to the floor and ran down to the living room as soon as she saw me.

Good move, Molly, I thought as I closed the door behind me. Now all the rooms on the upper floor were closed off to my shy little feline friend.

When I confronted Molly in the living room, she made a mad dash for the upper floor. "Now I've gotcha," I said. But my attempt to toss a blanket over her in the confined quarters failed. She leaped over my shoulder, hitting me on her way, and rushed though the kitty door leading to the garage.

The kitty door was a small ten-by-sixteen-inch opening at the bottom of the door that led from the kitchen to the garage. It was hinged at the top to swing both ways so the cat could go in and out of the kitchen at will.

I laughed out loud as I watched the kitty door swing back and forth. I knew confronting her in the garage would only make her dash back through the door into the house, and I was not inclined to play an endless game of cat and mouse with her.

The cat carrier was the answer. I propped the carrier with its door opened in front of the swinging kitty door on the kitchen side. Now if Molly tried to get back into the house, she would end up a captive in the carrier. I hoped it would work.

I went into the garage through the door from the backyard and spotted Molly in the rafters. A little nudging with a broom did the trick. She leaped to the floor and jumped through the kitty door. I quickly grabbed a nearby ladder and propped it against the kitty door so she could not escape back into the garage, and I rushed into the kitchen to survey my captive. Carefully picking up the carrier with Molly inside, I breathed a sigh of relief.

Nothing is as amazing as the feeling you get when you outsmart a cat—or when you think you did.

The Day Planner

Mile Marker 7,032

As guest speaker at a meeting at the annual week-long Families United Camp, one of my jobs was to encourage those in attendance to faithfully visit the local churches, share in the Bible study, and, in all ways possible, support the local church's ministry.

Camp services were held Monday through Saturday, afternoon and evening. On Sunday morning, the camp attendees were encouraged to visit churches in the surrounding towns and take their Bibles and pamphlets advertising the family camp activities.

I chose a small church a few miles from the campground. The church was packed, and the only seat available was in the back row. A few minutes into the congregational singing, the pastor saw me and asked that I join the other visiting leaders on the stage.

When I was introduced, I was asked to greet the congregants. I did, and as I turned to leave the microphone, the host asked me to read my favorite Bible verse. When I took my small Bible out of my jacket pocket, I was surprised to discover it was not my Bible but my leather day planner. Without missing a beat (and trying to avoid embarrassment for not having my Bible with me at church), I opened my planner and said, "One of my favorite verses is Psalms 27:1: 'The Lord is my light and my salvation; whom shall I fear? The Lord is the strength of my life; of whom shall I be afraid?'"

Before I had a chance to close my planner, the host said, "Dr. Winford, my favorite is a few verses down on the page. Please read verses 3, 4, and 5."

I froze. I knew I was in trouble. How was I going to get out of this mess? Did fear register on my face? It was as though all the blood had drained from my body. I was dumbfounded. Why didn't I have my pocket Bible with me? I always carried it.

The Road Scholar

Just then, an elderly minister seated behind me rose to his feet and, in a trembling voice, said, "I know those verses by heart. They are my favorite. Let me share them with you."

And he quoted them word for word, I think.

Whiskey

Mile Marker 12,111

When my plane landed at the airport in Minot, North Dakota, my heart raced. The flight was over an hour late, and the minister who was to meet me would be anxious to pick me up and get back to the rally where I was to be the keynote speaker.

For years, I tried to use my influence for good causes, and one of my causes was a battle against booze, dope, and weeds—alcohol, drugs, and tobacco. In fact, I had recently presented a program titled "Booze, Dope, and Weeds" in all the public and private schools in North Dakota and South Dakota.

On each flight, in those days, the airline would give complimentary, thumb-sized bottles of whiskey to passengers. I was and am a teetotaler, so I refused the tiny bottles of booze each time the stewardess offered. I soon learned an important lesson: Whoever sat next to me would ask for them, and on one occasion, actually got the stewardess to give him the bottles that were intended for me.

From then on, I took the whiskey, put it in my pocket, and later transferred it to my suitcase. The more flights I took, the more whiskey I collected. While speaking at churches and schools and staying in local motels, I didn't feel comfortable pouring the whiskey down the drain and tossing the empties into the waste basket. What if the maid attends church or has some connection with the schools where I appear and tells the school personnel or minister that I'm a sot drunk, I reasoned. It wouldn't be the truth, but it wouldn't be good for me either.

Soon my suitcase was too full for anymore whiskey, and I really had to get rid of the stuff, but where and how?

When the plane taxied up to the gate at Minot, I grabbed my luggage, hurried down the steps, and rushed into the terminal building. As I ran toward the door marked for ground transportation, I bumped into a pillar, and my suitcase spilled its contents all across the floor. In a panic, I fell to my knees and frantically began to scoop up my belongings and stuff them back into my bag. With the last whiskey bottle, pairs of socks, and unmentionables back, I slowly stood up only to see an old lady putting her hand out to me and saying in a faltering voice, "Hey, mister, is this yours?" In her hand was a bottle of whiskey. I grabbed it and stuffed it into my pocket, and as I turned, there stood the minister looking at me in dumb silence.

The silence lasted all the way to the rally. In fact, it lingered through the day. I looked for an opportunity to explain what had happened and that my mission was really a worthy one, but the chance never came.

To this day, that pastor and everyone he shared the story with probably thinks I'm a no-good boozer. Sobering thought!

My Big Gulp

Mile Marker 997

Traveling in the south on a special mission to promote evangelism, I was invited to a church in Arkansas. The church pastor was an elderly minister. He and his wife had been resident ministers of this church for many years. The congregation was small and finances were limited, so I was asked to stay with them in their home.

They had a spare bedroom for just such an occasion. I gladly moved in with my suitcase, stack of books, and promotional materials. My room was comfortably appointed with a bed, dresser, reading and writing desk, and a closet for the few things I brought. A long hall separated my bedroom and theirs. Halfway between our rooms was the common bathroom.

When I stay in someone's home, I always try to keep pretty much to myself and not interrupt the family's routine. This minister and his wife retired early, so I used the free time to catch up on reading. To make sure I didn't bother them, I put a small throw rug against the bottom of the door to keep the light from shining down the hallway. After reading for an hour or so, I turned off the lights and fell asleep.

One morning, long before dawn, I awoke very thirsty. I lay in bed for a while hoping to go back to sleep, but that was not to be. Finally, I slipped out of bed and quietly crept down the hall to the bathroom. I knew the couple was sleeping; I could hear the elderly minister snoring. Through the window came the distant sounds of crickets and other nighttime creatures.

Not wanting to wake the reverend and his wife, I didn't turn on any lights. The full moon cast an eerie glow through the open window. I turned on the cold faucet, let it trickle for a moment or so, picked up the cup, and filled it to the brim. As I drank deeply from the refreshing cup, something fell against my upper lip.

It was the parson's false teeth left to soak all night in some kind of foamy stuff.

One Hot Mexican Dish

Mile Marker 525

What does an eighteen-year-old know? Well, I thought I knew a lot. Since the age of fourteen, I traveled with various evangelists or musical groups. I played bass. Mine was a six-foot-three blond. We made quite a pair.

In travels throughout the country with my bass in tow, I had a variety of experiences, especially in the foods I ate. Everywhere I went, my host wanted to entertain me and treat me to the best restaurants in their town.

I'd sampled a lot of different foods, all except Mexican. You'd think by the time I turned eighteen I would have been to a Mexican restaurant or two, but I hadn't.

One day, while our group was playing at a tent revival in El Reno, Oklahoma, I hitchhiked thirty miles or so to Oklahoma City, the capital of the state. When I got there, I walked around and looked at all the sites. What amazed me most was seeing oil wells pumping on the state capitol grounds. Now that's capitalism, I thought!

Since I hiked more than I hitched during that thirty-mile trip, I was really hungry. So, finding a nice restaurant was the next thing on my agenda. In those days, fast food restaurants had not been invented. There were occasional hot dog or hamburger joints along with family restaurants, but nothing like today's variety of hurry-burgers.

I came upon a classy looking Mexican restaurant. The decor of the building screamed Mexico. Wow! I thought this place was hauled lock, stock, and barrel from across the border. There were landscape paintings on the outer walls depicting burros and sagebrush, tiny adobe huts, and a well, complete with a hand crank to fetch the water. That's all I needed to see. I was sure the inside of the restaurant would be unbelievable. It was. The waiters wore those big-brimmed hats they called sombreros and clothes right out of the wardrobe of a Hollywood movie lot.

I was met at the door by a beautiful senorita who led me to my table. Not knowing the menu, I asked the waiter for his recommendation. He suggested a meal I knew would be right for my empty stomach. He described the luscious beef, rice, beans, salad, flat bread, and all the trimmings in his best English. It made my mouth water, so what could I say? "Please, I'll take that."

He first brought a small bowl of what looked like cold soup. Since I was starving, I thought I would eat the soup and not wait for him to bring my iced tea. I took a big spoonful of the "soup," and that's when it happened. First, my mouth—the one that moments ago watered—caught on fire, and then, even before I could jump up, my throat and stomach burst into flames. The "soup" was not soup, but some kind of sauce—the likes of which I had never known.

I leaped to my feet and ran toward the "Senor" and "Senorita" restrooms. At this point, it didn't matter which one I got to first. I knew my life would be over before I got to either one.

Leaning over the sink with the faucet running full force, I frantically scooped water into my mouth with both hands hoping to extinguish the inferno. It didn't work. The more water I shoveled into my mouth, the worse things got. I didn't want to die here, but my best guess was I would.

How much water does it take to quench a roaring flame and keep it from consuming your entire body? Ask me!

You know I survived or I wouldn't be here telling you this story.

Hello, World

Mile Marker 319

Being a special guest at events across the country often puts you in an awkward position. You are expected to promote your program on radio and television and often with little or no advance notice.

This day in Muskogee, Oklahoma, things were no different. I was given the assignment to promote my appearance at a nearby church on a local radio station.

I parked my car at the curb in the middle of town, just a few doors from the entrance to the station. As I climbed the stairs to the third floor, it ran through my mind that I might be a little late and the pastor would start the radio broadcast without me. I had been given the station's location and told to be there by 7:30 a.m.

Little did I know, I was the only one to be on the broadcast that day, and the 7:30 a.m. program would actually start at 8:00 a.m., so I had plenty of time.

Out of breath, I reached the third-floor radio station and was greeted by the program director. She said, "You must be Bob."

At that moment that was the only thing I was sure of, so I said, "Yes."

"Right this way, Bob. We are remodeling the facilities, as you can see, so things are a little cluttered. We're opening up two additional broadcast rooms down this hall and adding new restrooms and a staff lounge over there," she said.

"You'll speak from in here," she continued, leading me into a small, dingy room with a table and microphone sitting on top of it. An old-fashioned hall tree (one of those useless things you see in museums) and a chair completed the furnishings. Hanging on the hall tree was a frazzled-looking chiffon scarf; I'm sure it had been there since the station signed on the air years ago.

"You'll notice, Bob, the station engineer is across the hall from you. He can hear you, but you won't be able to hear him. Your room has a double-pane of glass that will keep out a lot of the noise the carpenters are making as they walk up and down the hallway. Across the hall, the engineering room has the same type of double-pane windows. You will be able to see the engineer as he signals you to start," she said. "Try not to let the carpenters and others bother you. While you can see them, their noise will not disturb your broadcast," she added.

Lucky me, I'm supposed to do a religious devotional broadcast from the main street of Beirut.

I took my seat, pulled the microphone close, and waited for the hand signal from the engineer. The familiar three fingers, then two, then one, and I was on the air. Things went well for a few minutes, but the constant traffic of carpenters, station staff, and painters was a real distraction. If I could only block out the window, it would be easier to concentrate.

It was then that the chiffon scarf hanging on the hall tree caught my eye. If I could reach it, drape it over the microphone, and tuck the other end in my collar behind my head, I would block out everything. As I continued talking, I carefully and slowly pushed the table closer and closer to the scarf. My hope was that the table would not make any noise as I scooted it toward the hall tree and that the microphone would not fall off the table in the process.

Finally, I reached the scarf. I finished tucking it behind my collar and draped it over the microphone. Now I was safely cocooned in my own little tent. Things improved. My concentration was focused and I was on a roll.

As I relaxed, the scarf, without my noticing it, slipped from the microphone and, as I took a deep breath, was drawn into my mouth. As a natural reflex—in fear of choking—I bolted forward and grabbed the scarf, pulling it from my mouth and off my head.

To my surprise, the window was full of faces, some pressed against the glass to get a better look. Every carpenter, painter, and station staff person was there in my window wondering what in the world was going on.

In the distance, I heard the beautiful hymn "Just as I Am" and knew it was time to sign off. Looking into the faces of my audience of seven, I said, "This is Bob Winford. No matter how scary your life may seem, keep smiling. God loves you and so do I." The silent smiles on the crew's faces gave this new day a great start.

Itching for Fun

Mile Marker 1,297

It seems nearly a lifetime ago that we visited one of my favorite cities, Duluth, Minnesota. Our musical group, the Gospelaires, was invited to be special guests at a religious convocation headed by a famous team from Sweden. We were excited. The Gospelaires included Pete, Stub, Pill-Dee, Donnie, and me (Hawk). Those weren't our real names but nicknames we had picked up on the road.

As usual, we were on a very tight schedule, and the first service of the convocation would begin soon, so we had to hurry to get dressed.

Donnie, Pete, and I were staying at a beautiful tourist home. I was just finishing up in the bathroom when Donnie knocked on the door. I opened the door and started down the hallway toward my bedroom when he called out to me, "Hey, Hawk, is this your body powder?"

I went back to see what he was talking about and saw him holding a plastic canister of scouring powder the host had placed in each bathroom. I knew Donnie didn't have the foggiest idea it was scouring powder or that it was there so we could clean up the sink or tub after ourselves, and I wasn't about to tell him. "No, Donnie, it isn't mine. I used it and I'm sure you can use it, too," I said. In my mind, I could see him douse large amounts of the powder under his arms. He knew it would be hot in the auditorium and he'd want to be well prepared.

As hard as it was to keep the little secret to myself, I managed. The building was packed. The excitement was high and the audience was in step with the music. Everything contributed to a "Hot Time in the Old Town Tonight." The more we sang, the hotter it got and the more Donnie squirmed. I kept looking over at him and could tell the "body powder" was working. He scratched his armpits, loosened his tie, and finally took off his jacket. Beads of sweat dotted his brow. He was miserable.

I was consumed with laughter but couldn't let it out. Keeping a straight face was almost impossible, but I managed. During a break, I leaned over to Pill-Dee and told her about the incident in the tourist home. She passed the word.

After the meeting, we sat around the table at the restaurant and told and retold the story. We all roared with laughter—that is, everyone except Donnie. Somebody said, "Donnie, you're not still 'foaming' mad are you?" He wasn't, but chances are he was itching to get even.

Food for Thought

Mile Marker 13,006

In Los Angeles, home of the movie empire, there are some very touching human-interest stories that never make it to a movie script.

I was working as a strategist for a mayoral candidate in Los Angeles. At the end of a long and exhausting day, we stopped for a late night snack at a Beverly Hills restaurant. We had been working since before dawn and both of us were tired. He spent a couple of hours that afternoon in a hospital for treatment of a minor injury. The doctor told him he needed food and rest. We ordered club sandwiches, and after several minutes, we both decided what we really needed was to get to our rooms and get to sleep.

As I looked at the large sandwich on my plate, I thought to myself, I will be lucky to get one of these four sections down. I don't like to waste food, but I knew if I took the rest of the sandwich to my hotel room, I would end up throwing it away. So, I put the whole thing out of my mind and started talking about the events of the day and what we had lined up for the campaign tomorrow.

Steve had other plans for his leftovers. The waiter came back to our table and said, "I'll wrap this up for you."

Knowing that I would not eat it later, I said, "No, I'm finished with it."

Steve interrupted and said, "Take mine and Bob's and wrap them in three doggie bags."

I thought, He's got to be out of his mind; I won't eat it. When the waiter returned, he had three small shopping bags complete with fancy tissue paper sticking out of the top. Inside were six individually wrapped sandwiches, bags of chips, and napkins.

I didn't question a thing. We left Beverly Hills and headed home. Before dropping me off at my hotel, Steve turned down a dark alley and flashed his headlights. Almost out of nowhere appeared several seedy-looking people. When Steve rolled down the window and started handing the bags of food out to them, smiles of joy broke across their faces. I heard one of the men say, "Look, sandwiches and chips," as he shared them with one of the young kids in the group.

The Lord ministers through some of the most unlikely people in some very different ways. Before I got out of the car at my hotel, I asked Steve how he knew these men, women, and children would be in that alley. He said, "These street people are friends of mine. I take food and water to them every chance I get."

I walked to the elevator in silence with the words of Jesus echoing in my mind: "For I was hungry and ye gave me no meat; I was thirsty and ye gave me no drink." It was no surprise that when the elevator doors closed, tears welled up in the corner of my eyes—tears of joy, not for what I had done, but for what I had just witnessed.

The Clip Joint

Mile Marker 50,609

My older brother and two sisters were led to believe that our mother was in charge and she was always right, no matter what. I agreed. We'd be in big trouble with her if we ever expressed otherwise.

She told me to stop at the barbershop on the way home from grade school one day and get a haircut. I did. When the barber finished, I paid him the thirty-five cents he charged and hurried home.

No sooner had my mother inspected the haircut the barber had given me when she grabbed me by the shoulders and said, "Young man, come with me. We're going back to get our money. Your hair looks like stair steps. He ruined you." I wanted to die, but knowing that was not going to happen, I sure didn't want to be in that barber's shoes.

The three-city-block walk to the barbershop was frightful. While I was sure the barber was in for a lot of trouble, experience told me I had no idea how bad it would really be for him.

As a twelve-year-old kid, not many of my earlier prayers were answered. Today, I was sure both of my prayers would go by the wayside. My simple prayers were that she wouldn't kill the barber, but if she was going kill him, my second prayer was that she would kill me first.

When we walked into the shop, the barber was busily shaving an older man. Lucky for him, I thought, he's holding a straight razor.

"Is there a barber working here?" were the first words out of my mother's mouth.

"Yes, ma'am," he replied. "That's me."

In a louder voice, she said, "You call yourself a barber? Look at my son; you butchered him. I could have run over him with the lawn mower and done a better job." Oh, how I wish she had. I didn't know that was an option.

"As soon as I finish with this gentleman, I will shape up your son's haircut, or if you wish, I'll return his thirty-five cents," he said.

She shot back, "Thirty-five cents? I'd give three dollars and thirty-five cents if he had never stopped by this joint."

We left.

She carried the three dollars and thirty-five cents in her hand on the way home and plunked it on the kitchen table when we arrived.

My hair grew, but my love for getting haircuts never did.

A Dog's Life

Mile Marker 23,325

There she sat on her hind legs waiting for me to get home from school. The front porch was her favorite spot. She knew she could see me a city block or two away from that vantage point. She was a white dog, not more than a foot and a half tall. I never knew what breed she was, but that didn't matter at all to me.

The moment I entered our yard she would jump up, start wagging her tail, and run to me. I wondered, "Does she ever have a bad day?" If I had homework or things had not gone well for me at school, I sometimes would be a little depressed. Not Buzzie. She was always in great spirits and happy I was home, so for me, seeing my pooch on the porch was always a fun thing.

This was wintertime and playing outdoors was limited. When it was really cold, Buzzie and I would curl up on the floor and listen to the radio. There was always a good western or mystery show to entertain us. Television was out of reach for our family.

I remember one summer day, Buzzie and I were playing in the backyard. The garage, where my parents parked their car, had an addition on the back that extended the building four feet. I think this was an afterthought, because cars were longer now than when the garage was originally built. This addition was a little over shoulder-high on me, and that made it easy for me to jump onto its roof and from there onto the roof of the main part of the garage. Buzzie would follow me. There was a small wooden crate on the ground for her to jump on, then onto the lower roof, and then to the roof of the garage. She was surefooted. I had to be careful not to lose my balance and fall off the garage. It was a long ways to the ground.

One day, I had an idea. Because Buzzie was a fairly small dog and the family umbrella was large, I could fasten the "parachute" to her, drop her from the highest point of the garage, and she would slowly float to the ground. It didn't go well. Buzzie was ready and

The Road Scholar

willing to go through with my plan, but when she hit the ground with the umbrella smashing to the ground behind her, she was startled and ran under the car parked in front of the garage.

I hurried to Buzzie's aid. As I talked to her and assured her that everything was all right, she crawled out from under the car with the umbrella, now in ribbons, trailing her.

What a disaster! My mother was in the house. When she found out what I had done to the umbrella, I was going to be in big trouble. I looked at Buzzie and told her that when Mom saw this, she for sure would "tear up my umbrella." Buzzie seemed to understand.

How many times have I heard Mom tell the story of how I destroyed her beautiful and expensive umbrella? The story got longer and longer and more and more detailed as time went by. The last time I heard the story, I didn't recognize it or the kid who caused the crisis.

The Air Raid Warden

Mile Marker 50,289

World War II was in its heights. Our city was one of America's vital war production centers and under constant threat of being bombed by the Japanese. Aircraft engines, battlefield tanks, powerful artillery weapons, and related war materials were all manufactured within a short distance from our house.

To keep the residents alert and on their toes, the civil defense authorities trained air raid wardens. Their job was to patrol their assigned neighborhood and make sure the citizens obeyed the rules and regulations designed to help protect the homeland.

During an air raid drill, all lights were to be turned off in our homes and community. Streetlights, floodlights at parking lots and commercial buildings, and any automobile lights were to be extinguished. If a person was driving their car after dark and the air raid warning siren sounded, they were to stop their automobile and turn off their engine and lights.

One Sunday evening, our family had attended church services in a neighboring town. On our way home, the warning sounded. The shrill blast of the air raid warning could be heard for miles around. At that moment, we were on a long bridge and were signaled to stop. My father pulled the car to the edge of the road, turned off the engine and lights, and there we sat. I was frightened. Were the Japanese pilots going to bomb us? I was only ten years old, and I didn't know what I'd done that was so bad. I was pretty sure I hadn't done anything that deserved bombing.

It seemed we sat there forever, but it was certainly for a long, long time. Cars were lined up as far as I could see in both directions. Then the questions came: "How many cars will this bridge hold before it breaks?" "Mom, can you hear any airplanes coming?" Then the question that prompted her to tell me to just try to go to sleep: "Are we going to die?"

The Road Scholar

Another evening, when the family was all at home, the air raid warning siren sounded, and, as usual, all of our lights were immediately turned off—all except one. My mother wanted the radio on so she could listen for any news that might be broadcast.

In those days, we did not have television. No one in our neighborhood did. News broadcasts didn't last for thirty minutes every evening like today. News was broadcast at the beginning of the hour and lasted until all the news was covered, which was never more than three or four minutes. Today, the news always lasts no less than thirty minutes, and on some stations, local news can go on for hours. Network news channels broadcast around the clock, but then, "news" may be anything from dastardly criminal activity to the recall of faulty alarm clocks that don't keep time very well.

My mother cleverly put a heavy bath towel on top of the radio cabinet and draped it over the face of the radio, covering the dial completely. That was a good thing because the dial was illuminated by a tiny lightbulb, and my mother thought the Japs could see that light and probably drop a bomb on us. We all hovered close to the big boxy radio to catch every word of the news.

The Japanese didn't show up that night either, but it was still hard to go to sleep. My childish mind wondered if the war would ever end and why we had them in the first place.

Marvin

Mile Marker 70,289

My love for radio has led to many open doors in broadcasting. In my earlier days, I would purchase time on a local station to promote whatever project I was engaged in at the time: rallies, camp meetings, conventions, workshops, or just one-nighters at a local church, school, or theater where I would show a Christian film.

There are a hundred stories to share about these adventures; one that brings a smile and an important lesson is about Marvin.

During a short, two-year stint doing a radio show focused on politics, Marvin came back into my life. Our lives had crossed dozens of times through the years; this time he showed up at nearly every broadcast.

The audience often would erupt in spontaneous applause or robust laughter at remarks my partner or I made. I think Marvin was more taken by the waft of coffee in the air, the aroma of bacon on the grill, and the sound of eggs sizzling in a frying pan than anything else. He loved to eat.

The armchair politics brand of conversation, mostly off the cuff, took place in a local bar in Michigan. Being a teetotaler, I often felt out of place, but this show gave me the opportunity to express my conservative point of view and to challenge the liberal issues being discussed. I took the conservative side, and my worthy opponent—a professional debater and local attorney known for his strong liberal political philosophy and brilliant oratorical skills—took the other side of the issue.

More often than not, guests in the audience would stay after our sign-off to ask questions or give their opinions of remarks we had made.

Marvin had a more personal problem. He said to me one morning, "I'd like to know how you keep your weight down. No matter what I do, I cannot lose the pounds I've carried for years.

I'm three times the size of an average man my age. What do you recommend, Bob?"

With a straight face, I said, "Marvin, if you are the size of three people, feed just one of them and the other two will go away."

Obesity is a critical health problem for many people, and solving it is no easy task. Some people live with the crisis all their lives. With the scores of diet programs offered on television and promoted in other media, you would think losing weight is a simple matter. Subscribe to a food plan, sign on to a specialized exercise program, or try one of a hundred other solutions and you will be trim and fit. That's just not true. Some people have "tried it all" to no avail.

My hope is Marvin finally had an idea that worked. However, I haven't laid eyes on him since my stint on the radio show ended; I don't know if he lost two of his friends or I lost three of mine.

Snake Handlers

Mile Marker 36,444

We stopped at a gas station on the main highway to ask for directions to the next church on our schedule. The day was long, and now at nearly 6:00 p.m. we would have to hurry to the church in order to be ready for the 7:00 rally.

We asked the attendant how far it was to the Four Mile Pentecostal Church. As he wiped his hands on an old rag, he walked slowly toward the road and, motioning with his head, he said, "Hits four mile that-a-way."

As we drove in the direction he pointed, a makeshift, hand-lettered sign caught our eye advertising Four Mile Pentecostal Church. We turned right and drove up a steep grade to the frame church house at the end of the dirt drive.

The front door stood open. We backed up our panel truck as close as we could and started unloading our musical instruments. All seven of us in our troupe pitched in, and with months of experience, we could make quick work of setting up.

After emptying the truck, we moved it away from the building and went inside to plug in the amplifiers, tune the instruments, and get ready to start the program.

The pastor arrived and introduced himself. He looked unkempt and not at all like we were accustomed to expect. I felt overdressed. I'm sure everyone in our party felt the same way; it was too late for us to change our clothes to look more casual. I've been told about a thousand times, "The show must go on." Now I knew what that meant.

The gathering turned out to be much larger than I expected. This was a small rural church miles from the nearest town, and there was little evidence of the rally being promoted in the media—just a hand-lettered poster at the church driveway.

By the time the service started, most seats were filled, and long before we were introduced, the building was packed.

Then it happened: The minister led the congregants in prayer, and as he did, one of the parishioners pulled a small box from under his bench and took out a snake. Most of the worshipers were engaged in prayer; my eyes were focused on that big, big snake. When our leader, Dr. Belin, saw it, he gave a signal I'd never seen before: We were leaving!

We had to take down and pack all of our equipment in their cases. The triple-neck steel guitar, rhythm guitar, lead guitar, six-foot bass fiddle, large accordion, microphones, and related equipment had never been put in their cases and into the panel truck as fast . . . ever!

Setting up all of this gear took at least thirty minutes. We had to pack it all away and get ourselves into the truck and car by the time the prayer ended. My personal prayer at the time was, "God, help us!" He did!

I rode in the truck with Pete, and we couldn't wait until we stopped at a restaurant to hear what Dr. Belin had to say. All of us had questions for him. Dr. Belin was an educator, a brilliant student of the Bible, and founder of Pentecostal College, with a PhD to boot. A doctorate of philosophy is the highest academic degree awarded in the United States.

He carefully explained that some people had different views of sacred scripture and that we should not be influenced by what we had just witnessed. He did not endorse snake-handling or many other strange practices we might encounter during our travels, and he did not know that that the church we just visited was into that ritual.

As kids (Pill-Dee was 13, Donnie was 15, I was 16, Pete was 18, and Stubb was 19), we often talked about the new religion we had witnessed at Four Mile. None of us had ever seen such a thing before, so our conversation was laced with fear and disbelief.

What did the congregants think when the prayer was over and the visiting musicians were gone? After all, they came to the rally because it was to be a special occasion. Not often did they have guests from out of town, and certainly not from as far away as St. Louis, Missouri.

In our travels throughout Arkansas, Virginia, West Virginia, Kentucky, Georgia, Tennessee, North Carolina, South Carolina, and elsewhere, we had not run into people who brought snakes into their worship. I asked Pete, "Do you suppose we have been in churches that did have snakes but we were just unaware of it?" He didn't answer and I'm glad he didn't. That one snake was enough for me!

Me and My Big Can

Mile Marker 87,298

We had been traveling since early evening. No one paid attention to the gas gauge or whether we had stopped to eat. My tummy was empty, but in those days, with limited travel expense money, it was not polite to mention it. The car had no such morals. When the tank was empty, the car stopped. It did and we were at the backend of nowhere.

The car with her five passengers coasted to a stop. That sickening sound of the tires crunching against the gravel on the roadside told us we would have a long wait before we were on the road again.

The best guess we had was we were west of Effingham, Illinois. How far west, we had no idea. We did know that the last gas station we remembered seeing was miles behind us.

The decision was made to set out on foot in the direction we were headed—not all of us, but just one of us. I had a funny feeling who that person would be. Dr. Belin, our chaperone, and his wife both had on their Sunday-go-to-meeting clothes they wore when he gave the keynote address at the convention this morning. She was not the kind of lady who would walk endless miles in the dark of night to fetch fuel. Joyce and Geri weren't either. Two female teenagers alone in the dark were out of the question. So, it was my lot to start hiking.

Little did I realize it was as far ahead of us as it was behind us to the nearest gas pump.

The night was dark. Hanging above me was one of those eerie starless skies that sets the stage for a fear-packed drama.

My imagination ran wild. I could see the press statement now: "Skinny teenager found lifeless on bleak stretch of deserted highway."

I was scared. Just then, something streaked across the highway. A wild animal, I thought. Whatever it was, it was not alone. Another followed it. They were not used to a strange passerby invading their territory, and they didn't like it. Neither did I.

As I rounded the slight bend in the road, my eyes caught a glimmer of light in the distance. My heart raced at the thought of this being an answer to my prayers. It was.

Time has a way of dragging its feet, like yours do in one of those frightful dreams when you are trying to escape from a nonexistent assailant.

Once I saw the gas station, what should have been no more than a fifteen-minute walk seemed endless.

Pale and out of breath, I told the old man seated on a rocker out front my tale of woe. He listened patiently, and when I finished, he nodded directions and said, "You'll have to tell that feller in there; he runs the place. I'm just sittin' here killin' time."

I shortened the story and told the "feller" that my family ran out of gas and I needed to borrow a can and buy enough gas to get us back here. He obliged. He told me he had a one-gallon can and a ten-gallon can. Which one did I want?

I chose the large one, having no idea how much ten gallons of gasoline weighed. After paying the man, I braved the walk back to the car. What a miserable trip it was. I would heft the can, take a few steps, set the can down, and do it all over again.

As soon as I was out of sight of the two old duffers, I stopped every once in a while and poured out a little gasoline to lighten the load.

By the time I got back to the car, the sky was getting light in the east, but the can was as heavy as ever. There was plenty of gas left to get us back on the road and to the station. My fellow travelers never knew I had poured out most of the gasoline that I bought. They would not believe how frightening my journey was, so I never bothered to tell them. Let's keep it our secret, too.

The Four-Word Letter

Mile Marker 48,936

When Vice President Joe Biden leaned close to the president of the United States and whispered in low tones, "This is a big [expletive] deal," you'd think he would have had better manners. The excuse offered by the media was that the vice president didn't realize the microphones were turned on for the entire world to hear. Some excuse. It is appalling that today nothing is off-limits. Where is our nation's sense of decency and morals? Is it wrong to expect our leaders to set a positive example for the younger generation?

Profanity seems to be the norm. As a former public school teacher, I have a sense of responsibility. I am appalled at adults who have little regard for children and use profanity so much of the time. In some parts of the country, it is against the law to use profanity in public.

An acquaintance of mine, who is a very successful entrepreneur with businesses strewn across the nation, has one of the worst habits of cursing I've ever witnessed. It seems every sentence coming out of his mouth is laced with four-letter words.

One day, he asked me to visit him at his office. I watched as he leaned back in his oversized leather chair and held court with his entourage of hired hands who kowtowed to his every whim. His habit of spilling profanity was in play. Closely attended by his personal bodyguard, counselor, and two advisors, he was the center of attention and eating it up.

He had an aide pull up a side chair to his preferred position for me to sit; he said it gave him an opportunity to look me square in the (expletive) eyes. The chair was directly in front of him across from his massive mahogany desk. If bright lights were focused on me, you'd think I was being interrogated by the cops. They weren't and I wasn't.

I listened to as much as I could tolerate. To get his undivided attention, I suddenly leaned forward—hanging across his desk—and said, "I know where you were born," pointing my finger in his face.

Fascinated with my statement, he said, "I don't think you have any [expletive] idea. Everyone thinks I was born here on the west side of the city, but they are dead wrong."

I added, "But I know for sure."

He said, "Where, smart guy? You're such a [expletive] genius?"

"Vulgaria," I said.

The audience of four first snickered, then broke out in robust laughter. The tycoon didn't understand what I was saying or why members of his crew were laughing so hard and said, "Why in [expletive] did you say that?"

"Because you speak Vulgarian fluently," I said. By then, his staff couldn't contain themselves. One of them felt he had to explain what I was saying.

Their laughter faded in the background as I left his office. I thought, "He won't invite me back for a long, long time."

P.S. A short four-word letter to all thinking adults: "Kids may be listening."

The Coal Minor

Mile Marker 54,961

The tough years during World War II caused hardship for many families. There was a shortage of gasoline, automobile tires, and an endless list of necessities. One of the shortages was coal, the fuel our family and homes up and down our street used for heat.

While the economy seemed steady and jobs were plentiful, there was a severe rationing of everyday commodities; coffee, sugar, motor oil, and car parts were at the top of the list.

Most of the raw materials were dedicated to the war effort. The military needed tires for jeeps, trucks, and other personnel carriers. Steel was used for the manufacturing of tanks, guns, ships, and every imaginable piece of fighting equipment.

Our biggest need was coal. The temperature in our house was turned down as low as my mom and dad dared lower it. It was cold, and the winter months were especially hard to endure. Then getting the coal company to deliver a half-ton of coal meant we had to be put on the waiting list, and that could mean days or weeks for them to get around to us.

My dad could go to the coal company and pick up a small load in the trunk of the family car, but he was working at the defense factory and couldn't take off work to do it.

My mother had other plans. One day she told me she was going to take me with her to get some coal. She told me to get into the trunk of the car and keep my mouth shut.

She said when she got to the coal company, she would open the trunk and let me out to help her load our car. It sounded like a fun idea, even though I was a little claustrophobic. What I didn't know was when we got to the coal company, the attendant weighed our car and then waved my mother through.

She was instructed to drive around to the pile of coal and load into our car as much as she wanted. When she stopped the car, she opened the trunk and let me out. I helped her load our coal into the trunk, and when we finished, she told me to climb the fence surrounding the coal yard and meet her at the fruit market on the corner.

When she drove out of the coal yard, the attendant weighed the car again. By this time I was long gone and so was my skinny body.

I did as my mother told me and met her at the corner, but for several years, I was troubled by that sneaky ordeal. Do the math: My mother got about sixty pounds of coal "free."

Through the years I would remind her about that day, and when I did she just laughed. Shrugging it off as a joke was as wrong as stealing the coal in the first place.

Things like that make a lasting impression on children and serve no positive purpose. The coal company is long gone, so is my mother, but the memory is still a burning ember.

Barnyard Animals

Mile Marker 12,562

The kid across the street had an unusual family. He lived with his mother, grandmother, and grandfather. I always wondered where his dad was. He never talked about him, and my young mind never prompted me to ask. I figured he must work a lot like my dad did.

Paul Joey was sort of a rich kid. He had all the toys none of the rest of the neighbor kids had, and when his birthday came around, his mother always had a party for him. I don't remember anyone ever giving a party for me or, for that matter, the other kids that lived on our street.

We didn't know Paul Joey's last name. I remember hearing it once; it wasn't the same as his mother's or his grandparents'. By listening to older people in the neighborhood talk when they stopped by our house, I knew his dad hadn't been killed in the war. Who he was or where he was baffled the neighbors probably more than it did me.

One year, Paul Joey's mother asked my mother if I could attend her son's birthday party. My mom said yes, and when the day arrived, I walked across the street to join in.

My mother sent along a present for Paul Joey. I didn't know what it was; it could have been anything. I just hoped it was something nice and not some silly thing my mother was apt to give, like a secondhand baseball glove or some cheap trinket from the poor people's hand-me-down store.

The party was really fancy. Paul Joey's mother had gone all out. She made cupcakes, cooked hot dogs, and put out potato chips and individual bottles of pop. Back in those World War II days, there were larger bottles of pop called party packs. They were poured into paper cups or glasses and were cheaper than giving kids their very own bottles.

After we ate, Paul Joey's mom had all the kids go into the living room for games. I was shy and never very good at playing games.

The game she organized was called "Sounds of Barnyard Animals." She had all the kids sit in a circle, then went from one kid to another and whispered the name of an animal they were to pretend to be. When she finished giving each kid an animal, she said on her signal all the children were to jump up and make the sound of the animal she gave them. She insisted we should be really loud when we made our animal sound.

I was to be a rooster. That would be easy, I thought. I'd heard a rooster before and I could do that. Besides, all the kids would be different animals, and it would be fun to hear everyone together. I thought it would sound like a real barnyard.

She said, "This is the rule: On the count of three, everyone do as I told you. Ready? One, two, three!"

I jumped to my feet and shouted in my loudest voice, "Cock-a-doodle-doo!"

I was the only kid standing. She had told all the kids to not make a sound. I was the only one given an animal name. I was mortified.

I bolted from the room and out the door. I headed to my house as fast as I could run and went inside. No one was home, so I sat in the basement alone, feeling as bad as I possibly could.

For the rest of the time we lived on Knight Avenue, I avoided Paul Joey, his mother, and his grandparents. The other kids at his party were not my friends anyway, so I never saw them again either.

Phooey on birthday parties. Who needs them? The way I see it, they make you a year older every time you have one. Instead of parties, I'll keep practicing my rooster sound, hoping all the while that I am never again called on to use it. The fact is, I'm getting better at it every day. Just ask me.

Nightie-Night

Mile Marker 72,278

Being with Karen has always been one of the most enjoyable times of my life. Occasionally, I get to go with her shopping. That's fun, too.

The rare times we go to one of those enormous shopping malls that houses a variety of bookstores, electronic shops, and coffeehouses are the most exciting for me. Not that I ever consider buying the latest handheld cell phone or game device, but just keeping up with the latest technology is important.

I've been encouraged to upgrade my flip-phone to one of those expensive devices that can access the Internet, but I resist each appeal. So at the mall, I trail Karen on her shopping excursion.

At Christmastime she has a whole gaggle of gifts to buy. I tag along to carry the packages. It makes me feel like I am contributing to the festive event.

One item on her recent Christmas list was a pair of pajamas sold only in one of those specialty shops that sells mostly skimpy unmentionables for women. They are places that I would never go into alone, and in fact, I avoid them even when I'm with my wife.

I feel out of place. Most of the customers are young women shopping for lingerie for themselves or older people shopping for their daughters. We were the latter.

As we approached the entrance to the shop, I told Karen that I would wait for her in one of the easy chairs just down the promenade. I said I would keep my eyes open for her and catch up with her when she came out.

As I sat there, a friend stopped by and said, "What are you doing here at the mall all by yourself?" I told him that Karen was in the "nightie shop" buying some pj's for our daughter. He said, "Why didn't you go into the place with her?"

I said, "As old as you are, you can't go in there either."

He said, "Why is that?"

"Because," I said, "I don't think they believe in having grays in the millinery."

Hits the Spot

Mile Marker 44.930

No matter where you travel in the United States, the people are hospitable. There is a difference in that hospitality, but it is always there and appreciated.

I'm amazed at how diverse cultures express themselves as they welcome strangers into their midst. Some social circles want to take visiting guests out to a favorite restaurant for lunch or dinner. Others prefer the warmth of family and would rather serve a home-cooked meal. Then there are those who serve up their favorite concoction, whether it is a handmade gift, a special pie or cake, or sometimes the outgrowth of a treasured family recipe. The South is notorious for the latter.

While appearing as a guest speaker at a rural church in Alabama, the minister warned me that some of his congregants would be bringing home-canned foods that might be a little hard to look at, let alone eat.

He was right. Home-canned chickens have the look of a science laboratory specimen that sits on the shelf for occasional review by anatomy students. Then there is pickled okra in pint-sized canning jars—just enough to serve as a side dish for a small family lunch.

What blew me away was the pecan okra pie, the signature dish of one of the ladies of the congregation. Pecan pie is a favorite of mine. The okra I can do without. But the very idea that the two ingredients can or ever would be combined is absolutely unthinkable.

One evening during my Alabama stay, the canned chicken appeared on the bench near the front of the church. This was a special place for parishioners to leave their food contributions for the pastor and visiting guest. I chuckled to myself as I imagined the chicken was placed on this altar-like bench as some sort of sacrifice, but I didn't express that thought to anyone.

At the close of the program, the minister invited me to his family's home for coffee and dessert. When I arrived, what I saw sitting on the kitchen counter was the "sacrifice." Picking up the quart jar, he asked me to follow him to the back porch. There was a large trashcan. He opened the lid and poured the jar's contents into it.

Then he told me his story. "So often, people bring our family food that they think we will enjoy. It is very thoughtful of the parishioners to share with us. Some of the things are really good, but some are repulsive, so I put them in the trash. I have named my garbage can The Spot. When I'm asked what we thought of the chicken or pickled okra, I say, 'It just hit The Spot.'"

Dr. Bob Winford Profile

Political Consultant
Conducted more than 2,300 political campaigns
More than 700 candidates
Produced hundreds of radio and television commercials
Authored more than 30,000 political brochures,
Tabloids and newspaper advertisements.

Public Speaking
Under the auspices of North Dakota State University,
Lyceum Department presented:
"Booze, Dope, and Weeds," depicting the dangers of drugs and alcohol.
Wrote and presented "The High Roads of Europe,"
a cultural and political program depicting views of the people of
Austria, France, Germany, Italy, Liechtenstein, and Switzerland.
Other speaking events include: political rallies,
Conventions, and workshops.
Guest speaker aboard the S. S. France.
Co-hosted "Morning in America," radio broadcast,
Washington, D.C.

Photographer:
Miss North Dakota Pageant, 1969
Freelance photographer in the United States, Mexico,
Canada and Europe.

Education:
Bachelor of Science, Evangel College
Master of Arts, Eastern Michigan University
Doctor of Philosophy, Oxford Graduate School

Research:
Bodleian Library, Oxford, UK
British Library, London, UK
Evangel College Library
Eastern Michigan University Library
Gerald Ford Presidential Museum
Jimmy Carter Presidential Library
Library of Congress
Michigan State University Library
Social Science Library, Oxford, UK
Statistics Library, Oxford, UK
University of Michigan Library
United States Patent Office

Memberships:
American Association of Political Consultants
National Association of Scholars

Oxford Society of Scholars
Phi Kappa Phi Honor Society
Past member International Platform Association
Listed in Cambridge Who's Who, 2007/2008

In-Touch

Bob Winford

Post Office Box 190312

Burton, Michigan 48509

DrBobWinford@Comcast.Net

Sketch by Kimberly Perkins-Murillo.

Contact information available on request.